The Jubilee Guide to Rome

The Four Basilicas
The Great Pilgrimage

by
Andrea Braghin

Editors
Edmund Caruana, O. Carm.
Philippe Rouillard, O.S.B.
Niccolò Del Re
M. J. Coloni

Translated by
Carmela Merola

A Liturgical Press Book

THE LITURGICAL PRESS
Collegeville, Minnesota

ABBREVIATIONS

AAS   *Acta Apostolicae Sedis*. Vatican City, 1909–.

BR   *Bullarium Romanum*. (Magnum). Ed. H. Mainardi and C. Cocque-
         lines. 18 folio v., Leo I to Benedict XIV. Rome, 1733–1762.

BRC   *Bullarii Romani Continuatio*. Ed. A. Barbièri et al. 19 v. in 9, to Greg-
         ory XVI. Rome, 1835–1857. *Bullarii Romani Continuatio*, 9 v., to Pius
         VIII, with the inclusion of Benedict XIV. Prato, 1840–1856.

PL   J.-P. Migne, ed. *Patrologia Cursus Completus: Series Latina*. 221 vols.
         Paris, 1844–1855.

Cover Designer: Ann Blattner.
Cover Photo: Ariane de Saint Marcq.
Graphic Designer: Sandrine Winter. Typeset by Julie Surma.
Design of the Basilica Plans: Alessandra Patriarca.
Photolithography and Printing: Albagraf S.p.A.- Pomezia (RM)

1	2	3	4	5	6	7	8

Library of Congress Cataloging-in-Publication Data

Braghin, Andrea.
    [Guida del giubileo Roma.   English]
    The jubilee guide to Rome : the four basilicas : the great
pilgrimage / by Andrea Braghin ; editors, Edmund Caruana . . . [et
al.] ; translated by Carmela Merola.
        p.   cm.
    Includes bibliographical references.
    ISBN 0-8146-2535-5 (alk. paper)
    1. Christian pilgrims and pilgrimages—Italy—Rome—Guidebooks.
2. Basilicas—Italy—Rome—Guidebooks.   3. Holy Year—History.
I. Caruana, Edmund.   II. Title.
BX2320.5.I8B7313   1998
263'.04245632—dc21   98-24140
                                                                    CIP

Contents

Preface 4

What Is a Jubilee? 5
The First Jubilee 7
A Jubilee Without the Pope 8
The Fourth Basilica 9
The Disaster of the
    Sant'Angelo Bridge 10
Four Jubilees per Century 11
Assistance to the Pilgrims 12
A Grand Jubilee 13
The Regulations
    of the Rite 14
The Interruption of
    the Jubilee 15
A Popular Jubilee 16
A Jubilee for the
    Modern World 17
Extraordinary Jubilees 18
The Jubilee of 2000 19

The Holy Door 20

Rome, City of the Apostles
    Peter and Paul 22
Who Is St. Peter? 25
Who Is St. Paul? 26
The Tomb of St. Peter 28

The Basilica of St. Peter 32
The First Basilica 36
A Slow Reconstruction 39
The Maderno Façade 40
The Bernini Colonnade 41
The Pilgrimage of St. Francis 44
The "Pietà" Chapel 46
The Blessed Sacrament
    Chapel 49
St. Peter's Chair 50
Bernini's Ensemble for
    St. Peter's Chair 51
The Dome 54
The Baldachin 57

The Basilica of St. Paul
    Outside the Walls 58
The First Basilica 62
Restoration Projects to 1823 64
The Burning of the
    Basilica 66
The Quadriporticus 68
The Holy Door 68
The Baldachin and the Tomb
    of St. Paul 70
The Easter Candelabrum 72
The Altar of the Virgin 74
The Chapel of St. Benedict 76
The Chapel of the
    Blessed Sacrament 78
The Chapel of St. Lawrence 80
The Chapel of St. Stephen 82
The Cloister 83

The Basilica of St. John Lateran 84
The Foundation 88
The Ancient Basilica 90
The Present Basilica 91
The Central Nave 94
The Cathedral of Rome 96
The Cloister 98
The Papal Altar, Presbytery,
    and Apse 99
The Ancient Mass 100
The Baptistry 103

The Basilica of St. Mary Major
    (Santa Maria Maggiore) 106
The Miracle 110
The Central Nave 113
The Chapel of the Blessed Sacrament
    or Chapel of Sixtus V 114
The Confession and the Apse 116
The Pauline or Borghese Chapel 118

The Popes 120
Useful Information 122
Photo Index 124

PREFACE

The objective of this guide to the four basilicas of Rome is to be an aid to pilgrims who are preparing to undertake the trip to Rome for the grand jubilee that will mark the beginning of the third millennium of the Christian era. Undoubtedly, it promises to be a marvelous experience. The Jubilee of 2000 will remain one of the most significant and emotionally filled moments in the life of every Christian.

The intent of this "Spiritual Guide" is to be an aid in experiencing the pilgrimage. It is a reminder upon returning home to reflect on the serenity, confidence, and hope that the pilgrimage offered.

The purpose of this book is to offer in a few pages historical information of the jubilee as well as the architectural characteristics of the basilicas. In order to help the reader to understand this experience, the history of the art pieces is presented alongside passages from the Bible, the writings of the Church Fathers, and reflections of some renowned mystics. The guide also provides information regarding the lives of the saints and Christian art and spirituality.

"But as for what was sown on good soil, this is the one who hears the word and understands it" (Matt 13:23).

Andrea Braghin

Reading Guide for Sidebars

 Lives of the Saints Spirituality  Reflections

Explanations   History of Christian Art

The triple silver shield of Clement VII issued to commemorate the Jubilee of 1525.

WHAT IS A JUBILEE?

According to the ancient Mosaic Law, the year of jubilee, or jubilation, occurred every fifty years (after seven seven-year cycles). During that year the tillable soil was allowed to rest, alienated lands were given back to their original owners without indemnity, and slaves were liberated. To commemorate this Hebrew tradition, the Church established a year of peace and pardon. During this year a general indulgence was bestowed upon those faithful who invoked it with faith and who, in order to merit it, followed certain conditions.

The Hebrew and Christian celebrations have a major difference. The Hebrew jubilee was based on economic conditions and remained an ideal. The Christian holy year originates in the spiritual realm of divine grace and focuses on the redemption of humanity.

There is no evidence of a holy year celebrated prior to the one promulgated by Boniface VIII in 1300, even though a reference to the Hebrew jubilee can be found in St. Ambrose (*PL*, 14, 907). It is here, in the *Apologia prophetae*, that David defines the number 50 as *numerus remissionis*. The term jubilee can be found in other medieval authors such as St. Isidore of Seville (*PL*, 82, 222), and the Dominican Umberto di Romans (1267), but they remain only references.

Toward the end of the stormy thirteenth century, news spread by word of mouth that anyone who went to

Boniface VIII opening the Jubilee of 1300. Fresco of Giotto.

Rome in the centennial year of the birth of the Redeemer would receive an indulgence, as had happened, it seems, in the preceding century. The tremendous and unprecedented influx of pilgrims amazed the Pope no less than the reference to the presumed Jubilee of 1200. (In fact, no written statement could be found among the archive documents, despite the careful research ordered by Boniface VIII.)

"You shall not cheat one another, but you shall fear your God; for I am the LORD your God" (Lev 25:17).

Now after John was arrested, Jesus came to Galilee, proclaiming the good news of God, and saying, "The time is fulfilled, and the kingdom of God has come near; repent, and believe in the good news" (Mark 1:14-15).

The First Jubilee

The need to respond to and channel the extraordinary religious fervor of the moment led Pope Boniface VIII to promulgate the papal bull (decree) *Antiquorum habet* of February 22, 1300 (*BR, IV, pp. 156–157*). The Pope proclaimed 1300 a year of universal forgiveness for all those penitents who visited thirty times if they were Romans—fifteen, in the case of foreigners—the two apostolic basilicas of St. Peter's and St. Paul's.

Even though Boniface's declaration did not confirm a tradition, it did mark the beginning of the celebration of Christian jubilees henceforth. The poet Dante Alighieri, a common man desirous of cleansing his soul like all the rest, was among the two million eager pilgrims who crowded the Eternal City in that prophetic year of 1300. The most solemn memorial of that first holy year is vividly expressed in the *Liber de centesimo sive jubileo anno* of Cardinal Iacopo Stefaneschi. Its author traces a detailed history of this event, most likely at the end of the jubilee year itself.

Portrait of Dante Alighieri.
Botticelli (1444–1510), private collection.

Medieval bas-relief
representing a procession.
Detail. Basilica of
St. John Lateran.

A Jubilee Without the Pope

Boniface VIII proclaimed that the holy year be celebrated every one hundred years (*quolibet centesimo secuturo*). Already by the middle of the fourteenth century, at the request of the Romans, Pope Clement VI had reduced the observance to every fifty years. In 1342, a delegation of eighteen members chosen from the Roman nobility as well as from the middle and plebeian classes was sent to the Pope, at the time in Avignon, to offer him the governance of Rome and to request that the jubilee be reduced to fifty years.

The Romans secretly hoped that this occasion would induce the Pope and the curia to return to the Vatican, from which they had been away far too long. Clement VI agreed to the request by proclaiming 1350 the next jubilee year, formally announced with the bull *Unigenitus Dei Filius*, of January 27, 1343 (published, however, only on August 17, 1349). Among the reasons given for such a change were the brevity of life itself and the memory of the Hebrew Law.

Clement was further supported by the poet Petrarch, who, having become a Roman citizen and in agreement with the messengers from the Eternal City, reiterated and justified Clement's initiative in one of his admirable Latin poems. But neither the Pope nor the Apostolic See returned to Rome, and the Jubilee of 1350, which brought thousands of pilgrims to the tomb of Peter, did not take place in the presence of Peter's successor. Instead, Clement VI chose to be represented by two cardinals, Annibaldo da Ceccano and Guido di Boulogne-sur-mer.

Avignon, the papal palace. In the foreground, the Scale District.

The Fourth Basilica

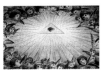

The *Holy Spirit*, Detail.
Basilica of St. Mary Major.

A further shortening of the occurrence of the jubilee was brought about by Urban VI, who reduced it to thirty-three years, in memory, above all, of Jesus Christ's earthly life. He ance with a provision of Gregory XI, who, in 1373, had added the Basilica of St. Mary Major (Santa Maria Maggiore) to the other three jubilee basilicas established by Clement VI.

Central nave, Basilica of St. Mary Major.

was moved by the hope that the new holy year, proclaimed in a schismatic climate, might put an end to the scandalous state of a divided Church.

For various reasons, the Jubilee of 1383 never happened, and Urban VI himself promulgated it for 1390 with the bull *Salvator Noster* of April 8, 1389. Celebrated under the pontificate of Boniface IX, it became the first jubilee in which, in order to acquire the indulgence, it became necessary to visit all four basilicas of Rome. This additional obligation was in compli-

It was Boniface IX again who proclaimed—without any document, it seems—a fourth jubilee for the year 1400. Only ten years from the preceding one, this fourth jubilee was attended with great fervor by the people, who wished to have a holy year for the new century. Also the penitents of the companies of the Whites came to Rome in great numbers. Indeed, they were so numerous that their name has been a synonym for the holy year, which has been called the "Jubilee of the Whites."

The Disaster of the Sant' Angelo Bridge

Pope Martin V proclaimed the new holy year of 1423 without an official bull and as a sign of respect towards Urban VI, who first decreed that the jubilee should be every thirty-three years. It was a rather irrelevant holy year due to the difficult times, as the accounts of the Tuscan humanist Poggio Bracciolini confirm.

The Jubilee of 1450, on the other hand, was grandiose due to the thousands of pilgrims who converged upon the Eternal City from all parts of Europe.

Proclaimed by Pope Nicholas V with the bull *Immensa et innumerabilia* of January 19, 1449, it was to celebrate the reestablishment of ecclesiastical peace. Unfortunately, it soon took on a funereal tone as a pestilence broke out in Rome. This jubilee's closing was no less disastrous, as almost two hundred people were crushed to death or fell into the Tiber on the Sant' Angelo Bridge. To commemorate those who died, the Pope later had two propitiatory chapels built at the beginning of the bridge, the Chapel of the Innocents and the Chapel of St. Mary Magdalene. In 1534 Pope Clement VII replaced these with two statues of the princes of the apostles.

The angels on the Sant' Angelo Bridge, placed as symbols of divine "protection" guarding the pilgrims' journey.

Four Jubilees per Century

St. Peter and St. Clement. Detail of the mosaic *The Triumph of the Cross,* twelfth century, Basilica of St. Clement, Rome.

Inspired by the success of the preceding jubilee, as well as by the consideration of offering every generation the possibility of earning the great indulgence, Pope Paul II, in the bull *Ineffabilis Providentia* of April 19, 1470, decreed that a jubilee should be held every twenty-five years. Furthermore, he specified that every holy year should go from one Christmas to the next.

This decision was confirmed by Paul's successor, Sixtus IV, through the bull *Quemadmodum operosi* of August 29, 1473. In fact, it was Sixtus IV who celebrated the first twenty-fifth year jubilee in 1475. The new ordinance did not attract an unusually large number of pilgrims, and in order to promote still further the jubilee, Sixtus IV ordered that all other indulgences be suspended during the holy year.

Since then the holy years have followed one another normally every twenty-five years, with two exceptions, 1800 and 1850. In observance of all the above-stated regulations, Alexander VI announced the new jubilee for the year 1500 with the bull *Inter multiplices* of March 28, 1499. With a subsequent bull, *Inter curas multiplices,* of December 20 of that same year, he established the inaugural ceremony, which is essentially still observed today. It consists in the simultaneous opening of the holy doors in the four patriarchal basilicas, carried out personally by the Pope at St. Peter's and by three of his legates at the other basilicas.

11

Assistance to the Pilgrims

In comparison with the importance attributed to the "grand meeting, principally of the northern Nations," which the Florentine historian Francesco Guicciardini documented, the ninth jubilee, promulgated by Clement VII with the bull *Inter sollicitudines* of December 17, 1524, was characterized by scarce enthusiasm. This jubilee marks the beginning of the coining of the commemorative medals of the holy year. During this period, the time of the Reformation, a large part of the Catholic world detached itself from the Church.

Decreed by Pope Paul III, but celebrated by his successor, Julius III (bull *Si pastores ovium* of February 24), the Jubilee of 1550 was characterized by the zeal of St. Philip Neri and of his Confraternity of the Holy Trinity of the Pilgrims. St. Philip and his Confraternity distinguished themselves by aiding and assisting all the pilgrims no matter what their origin. So great was their work that in the subsequent Jubilee of 1575 they not only continued their work but inspired other similar institutions.

The Jubilee of 1575, proclaimed by Gregory XIII with the bull *Dominus ac Redemptor* of March 10, 1574, took place at the height of the Catholic Restoration and was treated in the poetry of an epic poet of the time, Torquato Tasso.

The Good St. Philip,
Portrait of St. Philip Neri.
Church of San Girolamo della Carità.

A Grand Jubilee

The pilgrims who came to Rome for the Jubilee of 1600 numbered three million. This jubilee was promulgated by Clement VIII with the bull *Annus Domini placabilis* of March 19, 1599 (*BR*, X, pp. 504–510), which is an integrated version of the preceding one, *Tempus acceptabile* of October 30 of the same year. The first of these two bulls was essentially Clement's exhortation to all the bishops inviting them to come to Rome for the holy year.

Undoubtedly, this was the most magnificent of all the jubilees celebrated up to that point. According to A. L. Muratori, a historian of the time, its success was attributable to "the charity of the Roman Pontiff, of the cardinals and of all the people of Rome, an admirable charity evident especially in the many alms distributed to the pilgrims themselves and in the hospitality and generosity present everywhere."

Even though the jubilees of the seventeenth century were influenced by the pomp and splendor of the times, they continued to be examples of mercy and profound devotion, very much like the preceding ones. The Jubilee of 1625, decreed by Urban VIII with the bull *Omnes gentes* of April 29, 1624 (*BR*, XIII, pp. 143–147), introduced a novel practice. All cloistered religious, the sick and prisoners were given the privilege of earning the usual indulgence without having to journey from their respective residences. On the other hand, the fourteenth jubilee, solemnly celebrated by Innocent X after having decreed it with the bull *Appropinquat* of May 4, 1649 (*BR*, XV, pp. 628–632), was characterized by a severe rigor concerning strict observance of the thirty visits to the four basilicas.

In the jubilee promulgated by Clement X with the bull *Ad Apostolicae vocis oraculum* of April 16, 1674 (*BR*, XVIII, pp. 476–480), Rome saw the daily spectacle of continued faith celebrations in the solemn and picturesque processions of the various charitable organizations.

Statue of Pope Urban VIII, Museo dei Conservatori.

The Regulations of the Rite

The Jubilee of 1700 was obstructed by obstacles such as the Pope's death, the subsequent empty papal seat, and the overflow of the Tiber. Nonetheless, even though it was not a complete success, it did end up being all the things which a holy year should be. Inaugurated by Innocent XII, who had promulgated it with the bull *Regi saeculorum* of May 18, 1699 (*BR*, XX, pp. 876–881), it was concluded by his successor, Clement XI.

There was no lack of vibrant manifestations of faith in the jubilees that followed during the eighteenth century, despite the religious indifference present in the society of the time. The pilgrims who came to the Eternal City for the Jubilee of 1725 were many although not excessive in number. This jubilee was decreed and celebrated by Pope Benedict XIII with the bull *Redemptor ac Dominus noster* of June 26, 1724 (*BR*, XXI, pp. 53–59). Pope Benedict was most severe in prescribing the conditions for acquiring the indulgences.

In the Jubilee of 1750, decreed with the bull *Peregrinantes a Domino* of May 5, 1749, Benedict XIV took care to regulate again the holy year with four constitutions that established the ceremonial and rite.

The presence of pilgrims was rather sparse in the holy year of 1775. It was also the shortest holy year ever. Clement XIV, who decreed it with the bull *Salutis nostrae auctor* on April 30, 1774 (*BRC*, V, pp. 716–719), died on the following September 22. As a result, the holy year could not be opened until February 26 of the jubilee year itself, when the new pontiff, Pius VI, elected barely eleven days before, decided to publish again in Italian the promulgating bull.

The door of Santa Sabina. Detail.

Detail of the pavement,
Basilica of
St. John Lateran.

The Interruption of the Jubilee

The centennial holy year of 1800 was never celebrated due to several dramatic events, including the death of Pope Pius VI on August 29, 1799, who was a "prisoner of state" in Valence, France, at the time. His successor, Pius VII, was not elected until March 14, 1800.

As a result, the series of holy years celebrated every twenty-five years was interrupted, and another twenty-five years would pass before the twentieth holy year was proclaimed. Thus, the Jubilee of 1825 was proclaimed by Leo XII with the bull *Quod hoc ineunte saeculo* on May 24, 1824 (*BRC*, VIII, pp. 64–68). Pope Leo arranged to continue with this holy year in spite of the fears and worries produced by the political events of the time.

The Jubilee of 1825 can be considered the only holy year of the nineteenth century, for the so-called supplementary jubilee held in 1850 remains outside the official series. And even though the Jubilee of 1875, decreed by Pius IX with the bull *Gravibus ecclesiae et huius saeculi calamitatibus* of December 24, 1874 (Pii IX P.M. *Acta*, 1, 6, pp. 347–360), was considered juridically the twenty-first holy year, it never enjoyed the solemn unfolding of all the others since there were few pilgrimages that year.

A Popular Jubilee

The beginning of the twentieth century marks the modern rebirth of the holy year. The Jubilee of 1900, in fact, was celebrated in spite of the restrictions and hostilities of the time. Promulgated by Pope Leo XIII with the bull *Properante ad exitum saeculo* of May 11, 1899 (Leo XIII P.M. *Acta,* XIX, pp. 62–70), it observed the noblest jubilee tradition.

As with past jubilees, its success was assured by the large crowds it drew to Rome. The Jubilee of 1900 was brought to a close with a consecration of the twentieth century to Christ, the Redeemer. It received the attention of Giovanni Pascoli, who celebrated it in verse.

The Jubilee of 1925, promulgated by Pius XI with the bull *Infinita Dei misericordia* of May 29, 1924 (*AAS,* XVI 1924, pp. 209–215), enjoyed an even greater success than had its predecessor. The pontiff bestowed on this jubilee a special missionary character, displayed in the imposing Vatican Missionary Exhibit. The jubilee as well as the exhibit of that year represented "two great visions of faith and charity, two magnificent examples of brotherhood and reconciliation," according to the words of the Pope himself.

The Jubilee of 1950 confirmed and continued the grand character of the jubilees of this century. It was decreed by Pius XII with the bull *Jubilaeum maximum* of May 26, 1949 (*AAS,* XLI 1949, pp. 257–261). In order to acquire indulgences, the number of visits to the Roman basilicas, previously reduced by a third by Leo XIII, was further decreased to one basilica, and the time obligation was eliminated. The salient event of this mid-century jubilee was the proclamation of the Marian dogma of the Assumption.

Leo XIII,
Pope of the social encyclicals.
Tomb of Leo XIII,
Basilica of St. John Lateran.

A Jubilee for the Modern World

The last in the series is the holy year of 1975, promulgated by Paul VI with the bull *Apostolorum limina* of May 23, 1974 (*AAS*, LXVI 1974, pp. 289–307). At the closing of this holy year, Paul VI declared that "according to some, the cultural hubris, the modern mentality, the process of secularization that no one could stop, would compromise from the start the celebrations of this holy year. They constituted the obstacles to the idea itself of a Jubilee, wrongly conceived as an anachronistic leftover of the medieval world."

St. Peter's Basilica.
The left door.
The art of
Giacomo Manzù.

In reality, the Jubilee of 1975 produced more than satisfactory results. Large numbers of pilgrims from countries across the globe came to Rome. Furthermore, the participation of thousands of young people was one of the more noticeable and pleasing aspects of this jubilee.

St. Peter's Square.

Blessed are those who have not seen and yet have come to believe.
(John 20:29)

We profess our faith in a manner similar to that of bread-makers or doctors. Wherever we are, we're there not to donate our faith—for it is a gift of God—but in order to "explore" it within ourselves, manifest the content of its message, while tracing paths upon which it might tread. Our task is to be there, at the service of its source. . . .

We must not explain the matters of faith with the logic of reason; but with our reasoning, we should be able to say how to carry on life, all sorts of action, and thinking, so as to be able to remain within the logic of faith.

Faith allows us to come to know and love God. He ties us to him and by so doing, He lives within our lives and reveals this vital link. To conform life to faith is not only a way of filling the spirit, to believe is a way of becoming something else, not another, but something else (. . . .)

The presence of atheism has accorded us the opportunity of reliving, with a renewed and ardent desire, a practical dimension of our faith while accepting this faith for what it is, that is to say, the incredible possibility of knowing God in his existence and of loving him who loves us.

M. Delbrel

Extraordinary Jubilees

In the centuries-old history of holy years, in addition to the series of 25 regular or major jubilees, there have been 86 minor or extraordinary jubilees, 65 of which were universal, or extended to the whole Church, and 21 particular, or limited to specific countries, regions, or cities. During these minor jubilees, the faithful enjoyed the same spiritual favors and privileges accorded to regular jubilees.

Motivated by special or unusual circumstances, extraordinary jubilees have been promulgated by the popes when they felt there existed a strong need, as at the beginning of a pontificate, for a special need of the Church, or for the reestablishment of peace among nations, etc. They usually do not have a fixed time period. They can last a few days, usually 15, or, in some cases, an entire year, as was the exceptional case of the Jubilee of 1933, decreed by Pius XI to commemorate the nineteenth centenary of human redemption. It was defined "an extraordinary among regular" jubilees by Pius XI, who decreed it with the bull *Quod nuper* of January 6, 1933 (*AAS*, XXV, 1933, pp. 5–13). It lasted from April 2, 1933 to April 2 of the following year.

This extraordinary jubilee was followed by the Jubilee of 1983, decreed by Pope John Paul II to commemorate the 1950th anniversary of human redemption. Promulgated with the bull *Aperite portas Redemptori* of January 6 (*AAS*, LXXV 1983, pp. 89–106), it opened on March 25 and lasted for a year. A novel feature of this jubilee was the simultaneous celebration of the Redemption in the entire world and in all the dioceses, with all the spiritual benefits.

Statue of St. Paul.
St. Peter's Square.

The Jubilee of 2000

The objective of the great Jubilee of 2000 is the celebration of the 2000-year anniversary of the birth of Christ. In his apostolic letter *Tertio millennio adveniente*, Pope John Paul II emphasizes a further objective, namely, the formulation of a great prayer of praise and thanksgiving for the gift of the Incarnation of the Son of God and of the work of his Redemption. While the second millennium approaches its end, Christians are asked to take up again the themes of conversion and reconciliation, and to adopt the gospel of charity as a rule to be applied and lived daily.

The Jubilee of 2000 will be celebrated in the Holy Land, in Rome, and in the dioceses of the world. In his letter, John Paul II outlined a program that will unfold in three successive stages in the three years preceding the holy year.

Thus, the year 1997 focused on the figure of Jesus Christ, the Savior of the world, yesterday, today and always. It was the year for rediscovering Jesus Christ and one's own faith as well. It was also a time to become informed and sensitized to the significance of the jubilee and the mission of the Church.

The year 1998 is dedicated to the Holy Spirit and to the Church at a moment when the latter is called to testify to the faith in Jesus Christ. It is the year of the mission as such, in the community of the faithful and in the parishes.

The year 1999 is dedicated to the Eternal Father. During this year the mission will reach its culmination with the proclamation of the gospel in diverse places. During the unfolding of the mission, a continued and constant reference to the Virgin Mary will also take place.

The Holy Door.
St. Peter's Basilica.
Detail.

THE HOLY DOOR

The Christmas Eve opening of the Holy Door in St. Peter's Basilica, a ceremony that marks the beginning of the holy year, is attended by the reigning pontiff. It is rich in symbolism and is the most significant of the jubilee ceremonies.

It is not the key, in fact, which opens the Holy Door but the hammer which knocks it down, for the doors of divine justice and mercy yield only to the power of intimate repentance comforted by prayer. The Pope's firmly-held hammer symbolizes the power with which he is endowed, by virtue of which "who opens and no one will shut, who shuts and no one opens" (Rev 3:7). The knocking down of the Holy Door is followed by the Pope's solemn affirmation: "Haec est porta Domini"—

"This is the gate of the LORD" (Ps 118:20). The people gathered in the atrium of St. Peter's Basilica, who represent all the faithful, raise a shout of great joy as they answer: "Iusti intrabunt per eam"—"Through it shall enter the just." These same words adorn all the images of the Holy Door that appear on commemorative coins and medals. Among the outstanding examples are the triple silver shield issued by Clement VII for the Jubilee of 1525 and the medal of Julius III of 1550.

On the origins of the Holy Door, consult the following passages from the Old and New Testaments: Isa 38:10; Ps 107:18; 118:19-20; Matt 16:18-19; Rev 4:1; 3:20-21; Luke 13:23-25; Matt 1:13-14; John 10:1-18; 13:14-15; Phil 2:5.

The Holy Door, St. Peter's Basilica.

ROME, CITY OF PETER

Michelangelo Merisi da Caravaggio:
The Crucifixion of St. Peter, Church of Santa Maria del Popolo.

THE APOSTLES AND PAUL

Michelangelo Merisi da Caravaggio:
The Fall of Saul, Church of Santa Maria del Popolo.

From the very beginning, Christians have venerated in Rome the tombs of the two apostles of the capital of the Roman Empire. Pope Damasus I had the following inscription sculpted in their basilica:

"In this place dwelled, some time ago, the saints: you must know this, you who are seeking the names of Peter and Paul. The Orient has sent us these two disciples (of Christ), we testify it with great zeal. Thanks to their blood, which they shed in this place, they followed Christ among the stars until they reached the celestial spheres and the kingdom of those who fear God. Rome can therefore claim them as its rightful citizens. Finally, may it be permitted Damasus to ascribe them among the new stars of the firmament."

The oldest reference to Peter's tomb in the Vatican is to be found in *The Ecclesiastical History* of Eusebius of Caesarea, written at the beginning of the fourth century. Eusebius declares the following: "A man of the church called Caius, who lived at the time in which Zephyrinus was bishop of Rome (199–217), in his dialogue with Produs spoke of the place in which the remains of the two apostles had been placed: 'I can show you the remains of the apostles. You will find the remains of those who founded this Church'" (Eusebius, *Ecclesiastical History*, II, 25, 6–7).

Caius must have seen the modest monument at that time in the Vatican necropolis: a recess in a wall consisting of a niche topped by a small projecting roof or dormer, discovered during some excavations in 1945 and dated around the year 160.

St. Peter. Detail of a mosaic by Giotto: *La Naviella* ("The Barque"), St. Peter's Basilica.

School of Caravaggio: *Peter's Denial*, Vatican Gallery.

Who Is St. Peter?

The apostle Peter is the head of the twelve. His original name was Simon bar Jonah, which means "son of the dove," changed by Jesus to Kepha (Aramaic), which stands for "rock" or "stone." St. Peter came from Bethsaida. He worked as a fisherman. The only reference to his family is found in Matthew 8:14, Mark 1:29-30, and Luke 4:38. At first he was the disciple of John the Baptist; afterwards, along with his brother Andrew, he was called by Jesus (Matt 4:18; 10:2; 19:27: Mark 1:16; 3:16; 10:28; Luke 5:1-11; 18:28).

In listings of the twelve apostles, Peter is always named first (Matt 10:2; Mark 5:37; 26:37). He is always the first in authority, since he is always the one who speaks for the other apostles, and after Judas' suicide, he takes care to have him replaced (Acts 1:15-26).

Of fundamental importance is his recognition of Jesus as the true Son of God. For this reason, Jesus will change his name, declaring that upon Peter, "this rock," he will build his Church and will entrust him with the keys of the kingdom of heaven (Matt 16:13-20). Peter is also the first to ascertain the resurrection of Jesus (Mark 16:7; Luke 24:12; Luke 24:34; 1 Cor 15:5).

Given his own experience, Peter, more than any of the others, comprehended the repentance of the sinful person and the desire to be forgiven.

25

Who Is St. Paul?

"Meanwhile Saul, still breathing threats and murder against the disciples of the Lord, went to the high priest and asked him for letters to the synagogues at Damascus, so that if he found any who belonged to the Way, men or women, he might bring them bound to Jerusalem. Now as he was going along and approaching Damascus, suddenly a light from heaven flashed around him. He fell to the ground and heard a voice saying to him, 'Saul, Saul, why do you persecute me?' He asked, 'Who are you, Lord?' The reply came, 'I am Jesus, whom you are persecuting. But get up and enter the city, and you will be told what you are to do.' The men who were traveling with him stood speechless because they heard the voice but saw no one. Saul got up from the ground, and though his eyes were open, he could see nothing; so they led him by the hand and brought him into Damascus. For three days he

Paul, the apostle of the Gentiles. Medieval statue of St. Paul, Basilica of St. Paul Outside the Walls.

was without sight, and neither ate nor drank" (Acts 9:1-9).

"Three days later he called together the local leaders of the Jews. When they had assembled, he said to them, 'Brothers, though I had done nothing

Semicircular apse, Basilica of St. Paul Outside the Walls.

against our people or the customs of our ancestors, yet I was arrested in Jerusalem and handed over to the Romans. When they had examined me, the Romans wanted to release me, because there was no reason for the death penalty in my case. But when the Jews objected, I was compelled to appeal to the emperor—even though I had no charge to bring against my nation. For this reason therefore I have asked to see you . . . .' They replied, . . . 'We would like to hear from you what you think . . .'" (Acts 28:17-22).

After his conversion on the road to Damascus, Saul became the apostle Paul and his life was consecrated to the proclamation of the gospel in the Mediterranean region and in Rome. The Acts of the Apostles and his letters to the churches which he founded allow us to follow in his footsteps through the journeys that have permitted the world to receive the Good News of Jesus Christ.

The Tomb of St. Peter

The tomb of St. Peter is in the center of the basilica, on the axis of the papal altar built by Clement VIII (1594).

Emperor Caligula had a circus built in the area between the Janiculum and Vatican Hills, an area said to contain the so-called *Horti*, or gardens, of Nero. Subsequently, in this same area there developed a pagan burial ground mostly for freedmen. It was this area that became directly involved with the burial of the body of St. Peter. After he was martyred on the cross in Nero's circus, some Christians put his body in a tomb beside the place of martyrdom.

The exact location of the burial has been identified thanks to the scholarly research undertaken by Margherita Guarducci. A systematic study of the ancient installation situated under the Constantine basilica was carried out in the mid-twentieth century when a thorough inspection was made of the section of the burial ground near the Chapel of the Blessed Sacrament in the basilica.

Ordered by Pius XII on June 28, 1939, the research developed in two phases: the first took place between 1940 and 1949 and the second between 1952 and 1964. By the end of the 1950 holy year, the Pope announced to the faithful that the tomb of St. Peter had been found.

The burial place seems to have been subdivided into individual spaces by means of some letters of the Greek and Latin alphabets. The most important area is that known as *Campo P*, which is east of the papal altar. The area in question is delimited by a red wall which served as a partition for a space containing two superimposed niches divided by a slab of travertine marble, all datable to the middle of the second century. The structure has been identified with the *Trofeo di Gaio*, who lived at the time of Pope Zephyrinus (199–217). Guarducci asserts that the *Trofeo* indicated that a tomb was below it. In the excavations carried out between 1940 and 1949, the presence of a tomb and of a trophy placed on top of an

The Red Wall.
Vatican Crypts.

important area led the re-searchers to think that it must have been a tomb of an extraordinary person. Considering the date, it could only have been related to the tomb of St. Peter.

Nevertheless, in spite of the identification of the place with the figure of the apostle, the remains of the body were not brought to light, for the body of St. Peter received a second burial at the time of Constantine. In the middle of the second century, in fact, a room perpendicular to the Red Wall was built to house a cult of St. Peter. Today there remains only the eastern part of it known as *Muro G*. Again during the second half of the second century, another wall was built, *Muro S*, and some mosaics were added to cover it.

In any case, before beginning the construction of a new basilica, Constantine wanted to reinforce and secure the tomb of Peter. In fact, a parallelepipedo on a rectangular base was built, and within it were enclosed some parts of the Red Wall on which rested the *Muro G* and the *Muro S*.

A burial niche was cut into the *Muro G* and lined with marble slabs. In it were placed the remaining bones wrapped in a red and gold cloth. Given its importance, during the subsequent centuries, it underwent various transformations. The transfer of the remains from the earthen tomb to the niche was necessary to preserve the remains from the soil's humidity. It was this niche that was opened in 1941. The examination of the bones revealed that they belonged to a man between sixty and seventy years of age.

Subsequent excavations and research (1952–1958) led to the systematic study of the numerous epigraphs discovered in the earlier excavations. A surprising and fascinating graffito on the Red Wall contained the following words: "Here lies Peter."

← Detail from the inscription on the Red Wall: "Here lies Peter." St. Peter's Basilica.

The tomb of St. Peter, as seen from the Vatican Crypts.

Raphael: *The Liberation of St. Peter*,
Stanze di Raffaello.

"Father, all-powerful and ever-living God, we do well always and everywhere to give you thanks. You fill our hearts with joy as we honor your great apostles: Peter, our leader in the faith, and Paul, its fearless preacher. Peter raised up the Church from the faithful flock of Israel. Paul brought your call to the nations, and became the teacher of the world. Each in his chosen way gathered into unity the one family of Christ. Both shared a martyr's death and are praised throughout the world. Now with the apostles and all the angels and saints, we praise you for ever. . . ." (Preface, Feast of June 29 in the Roman Missal)

THE BASILICA
OF ST. PETER

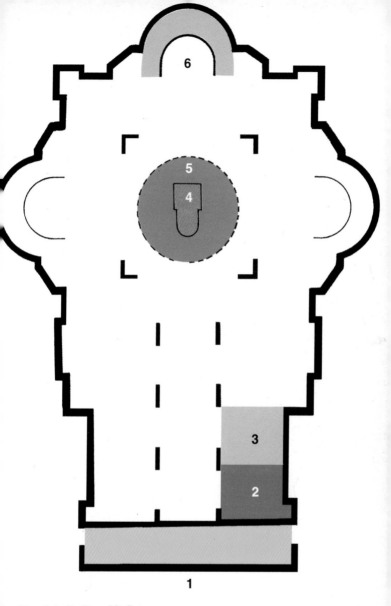

Plan of the Basilica of St. Peter:

- 1. The Maderno Façade, p. 40
- 2. The "Pietà" Chapel, p. 46
- 3. The Blessed Sacrament Chapel, p. 49
- 4. The Baldachin, p. 57
- 5. The Dome, p. 54
- 6. St. Peter's Chair, pp. 50–52

The First Basilica

The first basilica. Painting representing the medieval basilica, San Martino ai Monti.

The first Basilica of St. Peter was built over Peter's tomb near the circus of Nero, where he was martyred between the years 64 and 67, and following the express wishes of Emperor Constantine. Its construction entailed the filling in of the slope of the hill in order to obtain the space necessary for the foundations.

It was begun in 315, amid enormous technical, juridical, and liturgical difficulties. Pope Sylvester I (314–335) conse-crated it on November 18, 326, and it was completed in 349. This first basilica possessed imposing dimensions, comparable to those of the present structure. It was composed of five naves separated by columns. In the vast entrance hall with its four porticos, there was a *cantharus,* a tub used for ablutions, into which flowed the water that came out of the enormous bronze pine cone that today can still be seen in the Courtyard of the Pine Cone in the Vatican. The pine cone remained in the center of the porticos until the beginning of the seventeenth century.

The side of the porticos backed by the basilica was known as the *Paradiso,* and between the three windows of its façade there were mosaics commissioned by Gregory IV (827–844) and restored by Gregory IX (1227–1241). The mosaics represented Christ the Savior enthroned in the act of blessing. A fragment of this mosaic is preserved in the Museum of Rome. An integral part of the basilica was the bell tower, consisting of a large tower topped by a golden ball and a bronze rooster, the latter still on view today in the treasury of the basilica.

Detail of the door of the Ilario Chapel, Basilica of St. John Lateran.

In the interior, 48 frescoes of scenes from the Old and New Testaments adorned both sides of the principal nave. In front of the principal altar there were 12 spiral columns supported by a lintel, which was surmounted by statues commissioned by Leo IV (847–855). The statues represented the Savior among angels and the apostles. Finally, noteworthy of this first basilica were the five access doors: the Judgment Door, for the funeral processions; the Argentea or Silver Door; the Roman Door, used to post the signs of victory; the Ravenna Door; and the Guidones Door, named after the guides who accompanied pilgrims.

On the outside and to the left, in relation to the central nave, there were two buildings: the Chapel of St. Petronilla, octagonally shaped and covered by a cupola, with eight chapels and as many altars in its interior, and the Chapel of Santa Maria della Febbre. In later centuries, the basilica was embellished with frescoes, trophies, monuments and papal tombs, as well as tombs of the last of the Holy Roman Emperors. All these sepulchres, together with the tombs of many illustrious persons, have been placed in the Vatican Grottos.

"My life is consumed and distilled in this sweet Spouse, through this path, and the glorious martyrs through their blood. . . .

When the hour of Terce rings, I get up from the Mass, and like a dead person, I go to St. Peter's to work again in the small boat of the Holy Church. I remain there until about Vespers, the place I wish never to leave, neither during the day or night. . . . This body exists without nourishment, without even a drop of water, and with two physical torments which it has never had, in any time; my life is hanging on a hair. I do not know what Divine Goodness intends to do with me . . . but, regarding the physical torments, they seem to be the confirmation of a new martyrdom, in the sweetness of my soul, in the Holy Church. Therefore, it is possible that the Lord will raise me from the dead together with His Son, and will put an end to my miseries and to these crucified desires. . . ."

St. Catherine of Siena

Column of the ancient Constantinian basilica.

A Slow Reconstruction

Pope Nicholas V (1447–1455) resolved to enlarge and rebuild the apse after consulting the architect-humanist, Leon Battista Alberti. The Pope assigned the project to Bernardo Rossellino (1452). Work was suspended for over half a century following the death of Nicholas V, except for brief periods during the papacy of Paul II (1464–1471).

Julius II (1503–1513) decided to have the entire basilica reconstructed and entrusted the architect Donato Bramante (1444–1514) with the project. The first stone was laid on April 18, 1506, and work began on that same day. When a few years later both the Pope and Bramante died (1513 and 1514), the painter and architect Raphael (1483–1520) was called by Pope Leo X (1513–1521) to direct the construction. Flanked by two collaborators, Frà Giocondo (d. 1515) and Giuliano Sangallo (d. 1516), Raphael changed the original design from a Greek cross to a Latin cross. After Raphael's death, and as a result of the damages brought about by the Sack of Rome in 1527, the design underwent other changes.

The architect Peruzzi went back to the Greek cross, and then Antonio Sangallo redid it in the Latin cross. Then, in 1546 Michelangelo Buonarroti, the famous architect and painter, opted for the initial plan based on the Greek cross. Even though Michelangelo adhered closely to Bramante's first design, he modified it by making the building less complex and more elongated so as to appear less massive. Other changes included reduced dimensions and a new design for the cupola.

After the death of Michelangelo (1564), who had advanced the reconstruction a good deal, work continued at first with Jacopo Barozzi, known as *il Vignola*, and Pirro Ligorio, and later with Giacomo della Porta (1572) and Domenico Fontana (1585). But at the end of the century, for liturgical and structural reasons, Pope Paul V Borghese (1605–1621) opted again for the plan based on the Latin cross.

The stages of the construction of St. Peter's Basilica. Giovanni Frezza. Private Collection, Rome.

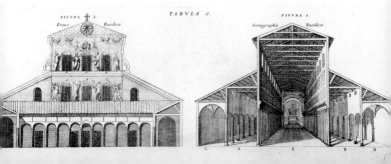

The Maderno Façade

The design competition for the façade of the basilica was enacted in 1600, and the winner was Carlo Maderno (1556–1629). Work on the façade was completed between 1608 and 1612. The interior portico was executed in 1619, and the roof covering of the longitudinal arm in 1614–1615. At the beginning Maderno followed Michelangelo's design. The change in the general plan resulted from a decision of the pontiff and of the cardinals' commission created to overview the reconstruction. The change was justified on the basis of developments in liturgical ceremonies. Furthermore, Maderno added three chapels on each side, pushing the nave forward, all the way to the present façade, which was completed in 1614.

On November 18, 1626, Urban VIII (1623–1644) consecrated the new basilica. In 1629 Giovanni Lorenzo Bernini (1598–1680) became Maderno's successor. Bernini completed Maderno's façade with the addition of a bell tower on each side, even though the first bell tower, already erected by Maderno to the left of the façade, had to be demolished because some cracks were found in the walls below. Finally, Carlo Fontana (1634–1714) succeeded Bernini.

Corpus Domini procession, anonymous artist of the seventeenth century. Museum of Rome, Palazzo Braschi.

Bernini's colonnade. St. Peter's Square.

The Bernini Colonnade

The square and the construction of the colonnade were carried out under the pontificate of Alexander VII (1655–1667). The final design of the oval-shaped square was approved in March 1657. The colonnade is 17 meters wide and is formed by 284 columns and 88 travertine pilasters. Each colonnade is 13 meters high. The entire decorative design was the creation of Giovanni Lorenzo Bernini, and the construction was carried out under the pontificates of Alexander VII (1655–1667), Clement IX (1667–1669), and Clement X (1700–1721).

The first appearance of a fountain facing the basilica goes back to Pope Innocent VIII (1484–1492). At that time, the Pope had a double-basin fountain placed in a space previously occupied by a trough. Its restoration was carried out during the pontificate of Alexander VI (1492–1503). In order to build a new fountain in 1614, Carlo Maderno had the old one dismantled, and using one of the basins, substituted it with a second one decorated with fish scales and resting on a stem. The fountain was placed next to the obelisk and was asymmetrical in relation to the façade of the basilica.

During work executed under Bernini's direction (1667), Maderno's fountain was dismantled and rebuilt with some variations, but it was aligned with the obelisk. The construction of the symmetrical fountain was completed in 1677. The second fountain differs from the first only in

The fountain of Carlo Maderno in front of the Basilica of St. Peter.

the decorative motifs and in the basin and stem. Both fountains were inaugurated in 1677, during the pontificate of Innocent XI (1676–1689). They were both restored in 1854 by Pius IX.

The center of the square is marked by a large monolithic obelisk. This red granite obelisk is mentioned by Pliny the Elder in the *Naturalis Historia* (1st century A.D.). It is 25.31 meters high, and its base measures 8.25 meters. It is the only obelisk in Rome devoid of Roman inscriptions.

Going back to the ideas of Nicholas V, Paul II and Paul III (1534–1549), Sixtus V had the obelisk moved to the center of the square in 1586, assigning Domenico Fontana as director of the operation. More than a century later, inspired by heraldic motifs related to his family, Innocent XIII (1721–1724) had two bronze eagles added.

In an attempt to complete the decoration of the square, Pius IX had four large candelabras placed there. Designed by A. Sarti in 1852, the candelabras are multi-faceted. In 1817, Cardinal Pietro Maccarini charged the astronomer L.F. Gilij with the execution of a sundial and a compass-card on the square's pavement, a design achieved through the use of the obelisk as a gnomon.

Statues of St. Peter and St. Paul are at the foot of the staircase. Sculpted by G. Fabris and A. Tadolini in 1838 for the new Basilica of St. Paul, which had been rebuilt after the disastrous fire of 1823, the statues were placed in St. Peter's Square in 1847, following the wishes of Pius IX.

The staircase leads to the wide enclosed plaza of the basilica domi-nated by the façade of Carlo Maderno (1607), who designed the atrium as well. On the walls of the atrium, six pilasters and Ionic columns create an appropriate architectural relief. The heads of cherubs that appear above the tympanums have been attributed to Borromini, who began his artistic career as a young stone carver in the construction directed at the time by Carlo Maderno. The floor, designed by Bernini, was restored in 1880 during the pontificate of Leo XIII (1878–1903). The central part of the floor was completely redone; it recalls the inauguration of Vatican Council II, celebrated by John XXIII on October 11, 1962.

Of the five doors which at present give access to the basilica, the middle one is the most ancient. Above it is to be found the Giotto mosaic known as *La Navicella*, which has been restored.

Giotto's mosaic *La Navicella*. ("The Barque"), Basilica of St. Peter.

St. Francis on the pilgrimage to Rome.
Portrait of St. Francis, anonymous fresco
in the Benedictine convent in Subiaco, Italy.

The Pilgrimage of St. Francis

In spite of his mother's tears, St. Francis, too, left his father's house and traveled the pilgrim's route to Rome to visit the tomb of the apostles. After traveling for one week, he went through the door of St. Peter's and fell to the floor, where he remained for some time praying with great fervor. When he got up, he noticed that the pilgrims had left rather paltry offerings for the completion of the basilica.

Before leaving his father's house, Francis's mother had insisted that he fill a large leather purse with gold coins. Since he had spent very little to feed himself during his trip, the purse was almost completely full. With an angry move, he opened it, letting all the gold coins fall to the floor, and attracting the attention of all who were present. Some people tried to snatch the coins but were blocked by the custodians.

Once outside in front of the basilica, Francis ran into a group of beggars who were asking for alms. Since he had no more money, he joined them and became one of them. Thus he came to know in a profound way the sweet spouse of his life: "sister poverty."

Christ the Judge. Detail from the Sistine Chapel. ➡
The Last Judgment. Michelangelo.

The "Pietà" Chapel

The first chapel that one observes upon entering the basilica on the right is that of the *Pietà*, originally known as the Chapel of the Crucifix. The present name derives from the presence, on the chapel's altar, of Michelangelo's famous marble sculpture representing the dead Christ reclining on his mother's knees, while Mary opens her arms in receiving Jesus in death.

On August 27, 1498, Jacopo Galli, representing Cardinal Jean de Bilhères de Lagraulas, signed a contract with Michelangelo that committed the latter to execute, at his own expense, a sculpture of the *Pietà*. His compensation amounted to 450 papal gold ducats to be paid upon completion of the work, set for the following year.

Upon realizing that the sculpture possessed the grandeur of a masterpiece, Michelangelo placed his signature on it, thus making it the only one of his works displaying his name. The Latin inscription "Angelus Bonarotus Florentinus faciebat" is sculptured on the band which comes down from the Virgin's left shoulder and crosses her bosom.

The painter-historian Vasari wrote: "Upon entering the place where the sculpture was placed, Michelangelo found a large group of strangers who were praising it. One of them asked who had done it, and another answered that it was the work of our Gobbo, or Cristoforo Solari from Milan. Michelangelo kept still, and it seemed to him strange that his labors should be attributed to another. During one of the following nights, having taken care to bring along a small lantern and a chisel, he shut himself in the place and chiseled his name on it."

> The iconographic theme of the *Pietà*, or the dead Christ taken down from the Cross and resting on his mother's lap, originates in the northern medieval popular tradition.

Virgin and Mother: The *Pietà* of Michelangelo.

The word "chapel" derives from the diminutive of "cape," from the name of the sanctuary in which the cape of St. Martin was kept. This particular use of the word was then applied to all the sanctuaries that contained relics, and the priest of such a place was termed a chaplain. In a larger sense, the word came to be identified with all places of prayer or worship that were not cathedrals. The word also indicated the oratories attached to royal residences.

47

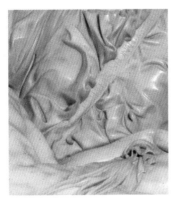

Detail of the band across the Virgin's bosom: "Angelus Bonarotus Florentinus Faciebat."

Benedict XIV (1740–1758) ordered that the *Pietà* be placed in the present chapel in 1749, after it had been moved from place to place various times.

The sculpture is 1.72 meters high and 1.61 by 1 meter wide at the base.

Since many reprimanded Michelangelo for having given the Virgin such a youthful appearance, the aged artist explained to Condivi that "such freshness and flower of youth as was preserved in her, as well as the natural way in which it was preserved, or her virginity, all combine to render more credible the divine power, which aims at manifesting to the world the perpetual virginity and purity of the Mother.

"The same process was not necessary in the Son; it was rather the contrary. For, in order to demonstrate that the Son of God took on truly, as he did, a human body, and was subjected to all those things in human nature, with the exception of sin, as any ordinary man, it was not necessary for the divine to hold back the human. It was merely necessary to allow the human to follow its course, and its own order, so that at the appropriate moment it could reveal its full nature."

In 1736, the fingers of the right hand were restored. On May 21, 1972, a madman armed with a hammer repeatedly struck the statue, disfiguring the face of the Virgin. Consequently, restoration was carried out by the technicians of the Restoration Laboratory of the Vatican Museums.

Do not repay anyone evil for evil, but take thought for what is noble in the sight of all (Rom 12:17).

When it was noon, darkness came over the whole land until three in the afternoon. At three o'clock Jesus cried out with a loud voice, "Eloi, Eloi, lema sabachthani?" which means, "My God, my God, why have you forsaken me?" When some of the bystanders heard it, they said, "Listen, he is calling for Elijah" (Mark 15:33-35).

The eyes of the Lord are on those who love him (Sir 34:19).

The Blessed Sacrament Chapel

Work on this chapel began as early as 1549 during the pontificate of Paul III (1534–1549). Among the art in this chapel is a representation, in the vault, of the Apocalypse amid a burning fire, and saints in adoration. Episodes from the Old Testament are reproduced in the vaulting, while the theme of the Eucharist received by those who are unworthy is represented in the lunettes.

The stuccoes in the vault, restored in 1758, were initially made by G. Perugino, following the drawings of Pietro da Cortona. The gilded bronze tabernacle that sits on the central altar, with the two angels kneeling in adoration on either side of it, is the work of Bernini (1674). The Trinity placed behind the tabernacle was executed by Pietro da Cortona. On the altar, to the right, is a copy of Domenichino's *Ecstasy of St. Francis.* The original is in the Church of Santa Maria della Concezione. The chapel is closed by an iron gate designed by Francesco Borromini (1629–1630).

The *Good Shepherd*. The Louvre, Paris.

In its literal meaning and original use, "eucharist" indicates the thankfulness of the person who has received a "good gift" and is therefore "grateful." Furthermore, it means recognition but also prayer of thankfulness. In a subsequent meaning, it signifies also the "body" of the Lord in so far as it is the pivotal point and the center of the eucharistic action of the Church in the visible forms of bread and wine. The reality signified by the eucharist originates in the Last Supper of the Lord (Luke 22:19; I Cor 11:23; Mark 14:22).

St. Peter's Chair

At the center of the apse is the monumental Chair of St. Peter. The present chair is in reality a grandiose container. The chair preserved within it, and protected by a bronze grating, contains another chair believed to be that from which the Apostle preached to the faithful. On February 22 the Church celebrates the Feast of the Chair of St. Peter.

Two of the twelve ivory inlays belonging to the Chair of St. Peter and representing the Labors of Hercules.

The chair was decorated with ivory ornamental motifs. A panel of twelve ivory inlays representing the Labors of Hercules characterized the front part. The chair became an object of veneration as early as the middle of the thirteenth century. When the construction of the altar was terminated in 1634, the chair was placed within a wooden container painted and gilded by G. B. Soria. The stonecutters Loreti and Balsamelli worked on the altar pedestal (1636–1637). In 1636, the relic was enhanced by a red velvet lining and enclosed within a gilded bronze container designed by G.B. Soria and G.P. Del Duca.

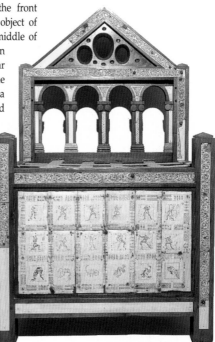

The ancient Chair of St. Peter.

Bernini's Ensemble for St. Peter's Chair

The design for the execution of a new bronze container was assigned to Giovanni Lorenzo Bernini. It was finished and used around the year 1645, but it subsequently disappeared. In the meantime, Alexander VII ordered a more dignified

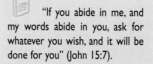

"If you abide in me, and my words abide in you, ask for whatever you wish, and it will be done for you" (John 15:7).

The Bernini monument containing the Chair of St. Peter.

preserving of the chair, this time in the apse. Bernini was again charged with the design, the execution of which he entrusted to his brother Luigi, since he was away from Rome at the time. But in the final stages of this work, a controversy arose concerning the chair's authenticity. At the heart of the dispute were the twelve Labors of Hercules, a subject which, at first glance, did not seem to possess any affinity with either the apostles or St. Peter. The dispute was finally resolved and the seat was proclaimed to be authentic.

It is important, nonetheless, to underline the difference in both the nature and the age of the elements that constitute the chair. The skeleton and the form belong to the eleventh century; the ivory strips inlayed in the front mirror are not easily datable, but they would appear to be from the sixth to the ninth centuries; the decorative friezes inserted in the tympanum, back and feet are from the eleventh century. Finally, the few wooden poles corroded by time and the avid hands of the faithful seem to have originated in the paleochristian period.

On January 17, 1666, the chair was placed in the monumental ensemble created by Bernini. It sits on a high, elevated base made of black and white marble from Aquitania and red Sicilian jasper. The four large bronze figures standing at the corners of the base represent the Doctors of the Greek and Roman Church: Athanasius, John Chrysostom (with the bare head), Ambrose, and Augustine. The top of the monument is completed with large

The term "chair" indicates an old or ancient seat, generally containing a back more or less high and curved without arms. The chair is usually made of wicker or wood, but the ones that have survived the ages and that we can still view today are sculpted in stone, marble, and ivory. The chair was widely used by both the Greeks and the Romans, who limited its use to furnishing baths, theaters, libraries and public spaces in general. In the Middle Ages, the seat of the bishopric was designated with the word "chair," from which it also derived the nature of its high dignity. The bishop's chair was generally placed on top of several steps, possessed a high back and was topped by a canopy.

angels standing around the glass enclosure containing a dove. The chair is further decorated with bas-reliefs and figures that represent the giving of the keys, the cleansing of the feet, and, in the center, "Pasce oves meas" ("Feed my sheep").

Bronze statue of St. Peter attributed to Arnolfo di Cambio, Basilica of St. Peter.

Love is patient; love is kind (1 Cor 13:4).

"If any of you put a stumbling block before one of these little ones who believe in me, it would be better for you if a great millstone were hung around your neck and you were thrown into the sea" (Mark 9:42).

The Dome

The dome, inundated with light, is built on four arcades whose vaults rest on four enormous supporting posts pentagonal in shape. The space contained by these structures forms a 71-meter perimeter. It was Pope Urban VIII who decided to have four colossal statues in the niches at the base of the pilasters of the dome. The saints within these niches include St. Longinus (with the lance that pierced the side of Jesus), a work of Bernini (1639); St. Helena (the mother of Constantine), sculpted by Andrea Bolgi (1646); St. Andrew (with his cross), a work of Duquesnoy (1640); and St. Veronica, by Francesco Mochi. Above them, Bernini made four balconies for the purpose of exhibiting the most famous relics, which include the Sacred Lance, donated to Innocent VIII by Bajazet II; Veronica's veil; the largest fragment of the Cross; and the head of St. Andrew.

Interior of the dome,
Basilica of St. Peter.

The Baldachin

Detail of Bernini's Baldachin, St. Peter's Basilica.

On June 28, 1633, Bernini's bronze baldachin, which is located in the center of the basilica and functions as the canopy over the papal altar, was inaugurated by Urban VIII (1623–1644). The imposing spiral columns, which repeat the form of the ancient ciborium, sustain a frame whose flowing pendants simulate the cloth contained in the portable canopies. Four angels holding up wreaths sit at the top of each column. The crown is formed by four volutes, which come together at the top of the canopy to sustain a gold globe, which in turn holds the cross.

Bernini's numerous and skillful collaborators included Duquesnoy, Giuliano Finelli and Borromini. Worth noting are the swarms of bees among the vine tendrils on the columns, the work of Bernini.

The angel is a superhuman being, a minister of God assigned to the human realm in order to announce and put into action God's will. The Greek term from which the word derives was used by Greek translators of the Old Testament to render the Hebrew term *mal'ak*, which means "messenger."

Pseudo-Dionysius the Areopagite was a master in the study of angels in the ancient Christian tradition. He defined the hierarchy of angels and delineated the three orders, each of which is subdivided into three choruses. From this definition derive the nine levels which, in a descending order from God to humans, are known as seraphim, cherubim, thrones, dominations, virtues, powers, principalities, archangels, and angels.

◀ Bernini's Baldachin.

THE BASILICA
OF
ST. PAUL
OUTSIDE
THE
WALLS

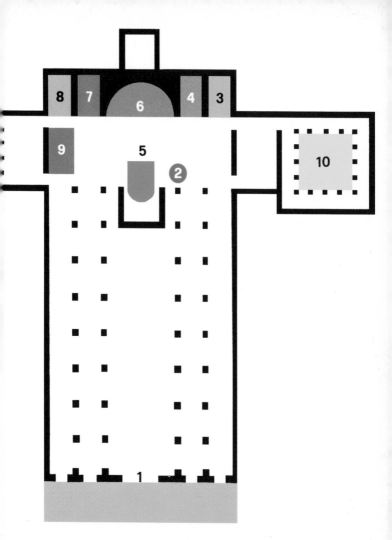

Plan of the Basilica of St. Paul Outside the Walls:

- 1. The Holy Door, p. 68
- 2. The Easter Candelabrum, p. 72
- 3. The Chapel of St. Benedict, p. 76
- 4. The Chapel of St. Lawrence, p. 80
- 5. The Baldachin and the Tomb of St. Paul, p. 70
- 6. The Apse
- 7. The Chapel of the Blessed Sacrament, p. 78
- 8. The Chapel of St. Stephen, p. 82
- 9. The Altar of the Virgin, p. 74
- 10. The Cloister, p. 83

Detail of the face of
St. Paul's statue
outside the basilica.

The First Basilica

From the first Jubilee of 1300, the Basilica of St. Paul Outside the Walls was included in the itinerary for obtaining the plenary indulgence. According to the *Liber Pontificalis*, the basilica was built on the *cella memoriae* of St. Paul, who was buried in a cemetery adjacent to the Via Ostiense, where he was martyred in A.D. 67. Built in 324, the basilica was a result of Constantine's wish to fulfill a request made to him by Pope St. Sylvester I (314–324).

Between the years 384 and 386, the emperors Valentinian II (375–392), Theodosius the Great (379–395) and Arcadius (377–408), the son of Theodosius who inherited only the eastern part of the Roman Empire, all commissioned a plan for a new edifice, which was completed under Emperor Honorius (395–423).

Emperor Theodosius the Great
(379–395). Badajoz, Madrid
Academy, Spain.

Central nave, Basilica of St. Paul Outside the Walls.

Restoration Projects to 1823

The head of Christ. Detail from the vault of the central nave of the Basilica of St. Paul Outside the Walls.

Before the entrance of the original basilica, there was a spacious atrium with a fountain in the center, and it had five entrances (compared to the seven of the present basilica). The first restorations took place during the first half of the fifth century, during the pontificate of Leo I (440–461). From that point on, restoration and embellishment projects followed one upon another under several popes: Symmachus (498–514), Gregory the Great (590–640), Sergius I (687–701), Hadrian I (772–795), Leo III (795–816) and John VIII (872–882). This last pope had solid walls built around the entire basilica to protect it from attacks by pirates, such as that by the Saracens in 846.

During the eleventh century, the basilica was embellished with two magnificent additions: the bell tower, erected next to the nave near the façade on the northern end, and the bronze door of the principal entrance.

Additional restorations and modifications continued under Gregory VII (1073–1085), Innocent II (1130–1143), Honorius III (1216–1227), Clement VIII (1592–1605), Innocent X (1670–1676), Benedict XIII (1724–1730) and, finally, Benedict XIV (1740–1758).

Statue of St. Paul from the Constantinian period. The statue is to the right of the façade of the Basilica of St. Paul Outside the Walls. ➡

The Burning of the Basilica

The fire that destroyed almost the entire building took place during the night of July 15, 1823. The carelessness of two workers who were restoring the roof seems to have been the only cause. Among those present at the site of the ruins the day after was the French writer Marie-Henry Beyle (1783–1842), better known as Stendhal. In his work *Promenades dans Rome*, he described the event: "I visited St. Paul's the day after the fire. There I came upon a severe beauty and a mark of misfortune which, in the arts, only the music of Mozart is capable of producing. Everything revealed the horror and the disorder of that fatal event; the church was filled with black steaming beams that were still burning; large fragments of columns split from top to bottom threatened to fall at the slightest touch; the large crowds of Romans present were dismayed."

Pius VII (1800–1823) died on August 20 that year, but he never knew of the basilica's destruction. The Secretary of State, Cardinal Consalvi, had decided not to inform him of the terrible devastation in order to spare him the grief which could have been fatal, considering the Pope's frail health. Reconstruction of the basilica was initiated by his successor, Leo XII (1823–1829).

A debate arose almost immediately regarding the dilemma as to whether the reconstruction should adhere to the ancient design or follow new architectural techniques. In 1824, the architect Giuseppe Valadier presented an innovative design, which he directed at no charge. It was completed in 1854.

In order to meet the enormous expenses, Leo XII promulgated the encyclical *Ad plurimas easque gravissima* (January 25, 1825), in which he invited all the bishops to inform the faithful of the need for their offerings. But on November 23, 1825, the special committee for the reconstruction of the basilica removed Valadier as director of the reconstruction and assigned the project to Pasquale Belli, promoter of a restoration plan.

During the pontificate of Gregory XVI (1831–1846), the architect Luigi Poletti, aided by Pietro Bosio, Pietro Camporese and Virginio Vespignani, replaced Pasquale Belli as director of the reconstruction. On October 5, 1840, Gregory XVI solemnly consecrated the Confessional altar, while a project for a new façade was approved in 1850.

Pius IX consecrated the new basilica on December 10, 1854, in the presence of 187 bishops (a large number for the time) who had come to Rome for the proclamation of the dogma of the Immaculate Conception. The mosaics in the façade were completed by Filippo Agricola only two years after the consecration, in 1856, while the vestibule was erected between 1873 and 1884 by Virginio Vespignani, the new director, who began the building of the quadriporticus (a four-sided, colonnaded atrium) planned by Luigi

Poletti. The paintings decorating the nave and transept walls containing the portraits of popes and scenes from the life of St. Paul were begun in 1857 by artists of the Roman School. Work was suspended between 1884 and March 14, 1890, the day of the laying of the first stone of the quadriporticus designed by Guglielmo Calderini. As a result of the rejection of Vespignani's design, it was not completed until 1928.

The final reconstruction was finished in 1931 with the installment of the bronze door by Antonio Maraini and the building of the baptistry in a room adjacent to the southern transept, a work of Arnaldo Foschini.

The basilica after the fire. Nineteenth-century painting by Diofebi. Museo di Roma, Palazzo Braschi.

The Quadriporticus

The quadriporticus, measuring 70 meters all around, is the work of various architects. Guglielmo Calderini completed it between 1890 and 1928 on the basis of an initial design by Luigi Poletti, which was elaborated by Virginio Vespignani after the death of Poletti in 1869. The northern and southern flanks are closed on the outside by a wall covered with travertine. The western side is composed of a row of 13 arcades.

The 150 columns comprising the quadriporticus are arranged in a single row in the vestibule, in double rows in the northern and southern flanks, and in a triple row in the front. Jesus in the act of blessing with the apostles on both sides is the subject of the 13 lunettes contained in the front portico.

Other decorations along the side walls have been decorated with painted medallions containing the symbols of the four evangelists and various paleochristian figures such as the vine, doves, the globe, deer, and peacocks.

"For it is a jubilee; it shall be holy to you" (Lev 25:12).

"You shall keep all of my statutes and all my ordinances, and observe them, so that the land to which I bring you to settle in may not vomit you out" (Lev 20:22).

When we speak of paleochristian art, we refer to the artistic period of the origins of Christianity, and the original forms both in architecture and in the visual arts which ensued from this period. This art developed principally in Rome and in the East. It flourished until the sixth century and has given us such important monuments as the catacombs.

Bronze door commissioned by Pius IX and executed by Maraini, Basilica of St. Paul Outside the Walls.

The Holy Door

The Holy Door was commissioned by the consul Pantaleone, originally from Amalfi, whose portrait is contained in one of the panels. It was cast in Constantinople in 1070 by the artist Teodoro.

The door, which was heavily damaged during the 1823 fire, is composed of six vertical sections containing a total of 54 panels. Within the sections, there are 12 scenes from the life of Christ (from the Nativity to Pentecost), the 12 apostles and the scenes of their martyrdom, 12 prophets, 2 eagles, and 2 crosses with Latin and Greek inscriptions. All of the scenes have been crafted in damask silver.

Right wing of the quadriporticus, Basilica of St. Paul Outside the Walls.

"Again I tell you, it is easier for a camel to go through the eye of a needle than for someone who is rich to enter the kingdom of God" (Matt 19:24).

"This people honors me with their lips, but their hearts are far from me; in vain do they worship me, teaching human precepts as doctrines" (Mark 7:6-7).

The Baldachin and the Tomb of St. Paul

Representation of medieval liturgy, Lower Basilica of St. Clement, Rome.

The baldachin is the work of Arnolfo di Cambio and his collaborator Pietro di Oderisio. Completed in 1285, it was commissioned by Abbot Bartolomeo, who was associated with the basilica from 1282–1297. The four porphyry columns sustain ancient trilobes in the form of pointed arches surmounted by triangular tympanums. Within the tympanums, pinnacles and angels sustain a rose window set on a mosaic backing. The bas-reliefs in the pendentives represent Adam and Eve, the offering of Cain and Abel, and Abbot Bartolomeo offering the baldachin to St. Paul. In the corner niches are statues of St. Paul, St. Peter, St. Timothy, and St. Benedict. The baldachin is topped with a small aedicule complete with spires and pinnacles. The decoration on the inside is rich. The decoration is principally mosaic with figures of animals placed among clipeus, some alongside cantharus. In the corners of the vault, there are four angels holding candelabra and thuribles.

St. Paul's tomb is under the altar.

"I will open my mouth to speak in parables; I will proclaim what has been hidden from the foundation of the world" (Matt 13:35).

"To you has been given the secret of the kingdom of God, but for those outside, everything comes in parables; in order that 'they may indeed look, but not perceive, and may indeed listen, but not understand; so that they may not turn again and be forgiven'" (Mark 4:11-12).

From the fourth century on, the baldachin was above the altars of Christian basilicas for the purpose of hiding the eucharistic service from the people gathered in the church. For this reason, the baldachin was equipped with side curtains that were drawn during the rite.

The baldachin of Arnolfo di Cambio, Basilica of St. Paul Outside the Walls.

Detail from the Easter candelabrum by d'Angelo and Vassalletto, Basilica of St. Paul Outside the Walls.

The Easter Candelabrum

The Easter candelabrum is a splendid example of the art produced by the Roman marble masters who, from the eleventh to the thirteenth centuries, gave rise to their own sculpture school and artistic trademark, which carried the name of St. Paul. The candelabrum is 5.6 meters high, and its entire surface is decorated. At its base, anthropomorphic animals are alternated with female figures. The trunk is subdivided horizontally into six sections. The first as well as the last two sections are decorated with vegetable and animal motifs.

The other sections contain scenes from the life of Christ. The principal scenes include Christ in front of Caiaphas, the derision of Christ, Christ before Pilate, Pilate washing his hands, the crucifixion, resurrection, and ascension.

At the very top, the basin for the candle is held by deformed animals. The tie with the paleochristian tradition and the new Romanesque culture is evident enough. An inscription placed under the cycle of the life of Christ reveals the identity of the two sculptors, Nicola d'Angelo and Pietro Vassalletto.

"I will keep the Passover at your house with my disciples. . . . Truly I tell you, one of you will betray me" (Matt. 26:18, 21).

"For the Son of Man goes as it is written of him, but woe to that one by whom the Son of Man is betrayed! It would have been better for that one not to have been born" (Mark 14:21).

This type of candelabrum was created in order to hold the Easter candle close to the altar on the gospel side. Beginning in the tenth century, it became a fundamental element in the liturgy of Holy Saturday.

Detail from the Easter candelabrum by d'Angelo and Vassalletto, Basilica of St. Paul Outside the Walls.

Medieval liturgy, Lower Basilica of St. Clement, Rome.

Lucas Cranach: *The Virgin with the Child Jesus.* 1529. Kunstmuseum, Basel.

The Altar of the Virgin

The altar of the Assumption has four Corinthian columns sustained by lintels with inscriptions. The statues on the right and left are, respectively, St. Scholastica, by Felice Baini, and St. Benedict, by Filippo Gnaccarini. The statues flank the mosaic made by the Vatican Studio, which reproduced the Assumption of the Madonna, a painting by Giulio Romano and dal Penni based on the drawing of Raphael preserved in the Pinacoteca Vaticana.

Once the earthly life of the Virgin Mary came to the end, she rose to the heavenly glory with both her soul and her body. Such theological doctrine was elaborated by the scholastics and subsequent theologians. The dogma of the Immaculate Conception was defined in 1854. Pius XII (1939–1958) defined the dogma of Mary's bodily Assumption with the dogmatic constitution *Munificentissimus Deus* on November 1, 1950.

The Altar of the Virgin, Basilica of St. Paul Outside the Walls.

"Love the most holy Virgin with great tenderness. Lay your trust in the protection of the Mother of God, and invoke her with steadfastness and humility" (P. P. Castroverde, *Spiritual Progress*).

"Hail Mary, full of grace . . . ."

The Chapel of St. Benedict

The Chapel of St. Benedict, built by Luigi Poletti in the right transept, was completed in the years 1843–1845. It has a rectangular plan (17.67 x 8.50 m.) and is decorated with 12 marble columns found in the ancient Veio complex near the Farnese Island during the 1811–1812 excavations.

The columns were acquired by Leo XII in 1824 and donated to the basilica by Gregory XVI in 1835. They are 2.9 meters high, and 11 of them have original composite capitals adorned with flowers and foliage. Only one is an imitation. The statue of St. Benedict made by Pietro Tenerani (1789–1869) is located in the niche behind the altar.

After the eighth century, the Basilica of St. Paul Outside the Walls was under the auspices of a Benedictine community that occupied the monastery attached to it.

"And everyone who has left houses or brothers or sisters or father or mother or children or fields, for my name's sake, will receive a hundredfold, and will inherit eternal life" (Matt 19:29).

Chapel of St. Benedict.
Statue of St. Benedict, patron of Europe,
Basilica of St. Paul Outside the Walls.

St. Benedict was born in Norcia, near Rome, about the year 480; he died at Monte Cassino in about 547. The few details we know about his life have come down to us through Gregory the Great. Benedict studied in Rome, but the dissolute life of the city turned him towards the more deserted and inhospitable places inland. He became a hermit, living in Subiaco until a community of monks asked him to become their abbot. Subsequently, some of the monks who thought his discipline to be excessively rigorous attempted to poison him. St. Benedict then returned to Subiaco and created twelve small communities in different locations.

In 529, he founded the monastery of Monte Cassino. It was here that he composed his famous monastic *Rule,* which incorporates preceding *Rules,* specifically those of St. John Cassian and St. Basil. He died standing up, supported by his disciples, and was buried in the same tomb with his sister, St. Scholastica. Pope Paul VI declared him patron saint of Europe.

His emblems include a broken cup and a crow. According to tradition, a cup containing poisoned wine was brought to him, but instead of drinking from it, St. Benedict blessed it, whereupon it broke! Tradition also held that St. Benedict had a crow which fell dead upon snatching the poisoned bread which his enemies had placed on the table before him. In this manner his life was spared.

Chapel of St. Benedict.
Statue of St. Benedict, patron of Europe.
Detail.

The Chapel of the Blessed Sacrament

The Chapel of the Blessed Sacrament was built for the Jubilee of 1725 with the specific purpose of housing the four-teenth-century crucifix erroneously at-tributed to Pietro Cavallini by Vasari. In the niches there are four golden-stuc-coed angels as well as a statue of St. Paul, scratched by pilgrims in an attempt to take pieces of it as relics, and a statue of St. Brigid, attributed to Stefano Maderno (1576–1636). Brigid is represented kneel-ing in front of the crucifix, which, ac-cording to tradition, turned its head towards her while she, prostrate at its feet, was absorbed in prayer.

Crucifix attributed to Cavallini,
Chapel of the Blessed Sacrament.

St. Brigid of Sweden (1303–1373) came from an aristo-cratic family. She turned her house into a meeting place for scholars and theologians, who, in turn, had an enormous influence on her mysti-cism. After her husband's death, she began to have visions, which she recorded in writing along with the things which Christ revealed to her.

Her founding of the Order of the Most Holy Savior (Brigettines) be-longs to this period. She came to Rome in order to obtain approval of the Order and she remained in the city of Peter and Paul until her death. Today the church dedicated to her is in the Piazza Farnese. She was proclaimed a saint by Pope Boniface IX in 1391, and her feast day is Oc-tober 8.

"Our life is love. If to live is to love, then hatred is equal to death" (St. Augustine, PL 36, 633).

Stefano
Maderno,
St. Brigid.
Altar niche.

Portrait of Ignatius of Loyola and Pope Paul III, Jesuit General Curia, Rome.

St. Ignatius of Loyola

Unable to settle in Jerusalem as promised, St. Ignatius and his followers understood that God wanted them in Rome, close to the Pope. His followers pronounced their vows in this chapel in front of St. Ignatius, who was intent upon finalizing the Constitution of the first Jesuits.

"The year was coming to a close, and since he had been unable to go on board, he decided to go to Rome. They arrived in Rome in three or more groups. The pilgrim, who was with Favre and Lainez, was visited by God in a very special way during this trip. After his ordination, he had decided to spend the first year without saying Mass, preparing himself and praying to the Blessed Lady who had united him to her Son. One day he found himself in a church about a mile outside of Rome. While at prayer in this place, he experienced such a change in his soul that he saw clearly that God the Father was uniting him to Christ his Son. He had no courage to doubt: he was certain that God the Father was uniting him to his Son."

The Chapel of St. Lawrence

This chapel was built by Carlo Maderno in 1619–1620 on the site of an ancient chapel dedicated to the Blessed Sacrament. The restoration that followed the fire was completed in 1852. The vault was decorated by Arturo Viligiardi (1869–1939) at the beginning of the century, with scenes from the life of St. Lawrence. The choir stalls placed along the walls were designed by Calderini and executed by the Perugian inlayer Monteneri. On the backings of the stalls are represented, in addition to architectural compositions, two of the twelve apostles.

The marble ornamental hanging on the back of the altar dates from about the end of the third century and the first quarter of the fifth century. Originally, it was in the counterfaçade of the basilica. The sculptural reliefs in its three niches represent the saints Antony the Abbot, Dionysius, and Justina.

One of the seven Deacons of Rome, St. Lawrence died a martyr in 258, four days after the martyrdom of Pope Sixtus II (257 or 258). He was buried in the cemetery on the road to Tivoli, in the place where the Church of St. Lawrence Outside the Walls is today. When the prefect of the city asked him to hand over all the treasures of the Church, he gathered all the poor and the sick and presented them to him. He was condemned to die on a grill, burned alive, even if, like Sixtus II, he was probably put to death by decapitation.

His emblem is, appropriately, a grill.

"No one has greater love than this, to lay down one's life for one's friends" (John 15:13).

And Jesus said to them, "You will all become deserters; for it is written, 'I will strike the shepherd and the sheep will be scattered'" (Mark 14:27).

Chapel of the Conversion of St. Paul, Basilica of St. Paul Outside the Walls. ➡

The Chapel of St. Stephen

This chapel, as well, was built by Luigi Poletti. The marble decoration of the walls, achieved through the partial use of materials belonging to the ancient basilica, was completed in 1847. It has a rectangular shape and its walls are marked by red granite pilasters. The altar statue of St. Stephen was made by Rinaldo Rinaldi. The paintings in the center of the side walls were commissioned by Gregory XVI (1831–1846).

After having been falsely accused by a few men instigated, in turn, by members of various synagogues (Acts 6:8-11), St. Stephen was brought before the Sanhedrin. He was interrogated by the high priest and found guilty of blasphemy. After being physically assaulted, he was led outside the city and stoned to death (Acts 7:58-59).

Chapel of St. Lawrence,
Basilica of St. Paul Outside the Walls.

Cloister of St. Paul Outside the Walls.

The Cloister

The cloister is situated next to the southern transept of the Basilica of St. Paul. A unique example of cosmatesque art, it constitutes a precious representation of ancient monastic environments. The four covered walkways encircle the garden, which is accessible from all sides. The walkways are delimited by a podium with columns disposed in pairs. Each span contains four pairs of columns, which further sustain small pointed arches. A pediment running on top of all the arches and decorated with mosaics is completed by a splendid framework.

The northern side (adjacent to the basilica) stands out from the others by the continued variations of the small

columns: smooth, spiral, fluted, intertwined and often decorated with mosaics. This clearly testifies that the cloister was executed by two different hands and at different times. From the inscriptions along the lintel of the east, west, and south sides, we know that the cloister was begun as a result of the express wishes of Cardinal Pietro de Capua and completed between 1212 and 1235, following the orders of Giovanni Caetani, abbot of the monastery at the basilica. The northern side seems to have been done at a later time in comparison to the other three sides and to the Basilica of St. John Lateran, with which it shares some features. It has been attributed to Vasselletto's son, who had to complete the cloister initiated by his father, identified as Pietro, the maker of the celebrated Easter candelabrum inside the basilica.

Many doubts prevail regarding the makers of the remaining sides of the cloister. They could have been Pietro de Maria, Pietro Vassalletto, or Nicola d'Angelo.

The statues which flank the Altar of the Conversion of St. Paul are of St. Gregory the Great, made by Francesco Massimiliano Laboureur, and St. Bernard, made by Achille Stocchi in 1836. St. Paul's conversion is the subject of the altar painting made by Vincenzo Camuccini. The altar table was a donation of Czar Nicholas (1825–1855) and is composed of malachite and lapis lazuli, flanked by gilded bronze angels.

". . . the witnesses laid their coats at the feet of a young man named Saul. While they were stoning Stephen . . . ." (Acts 7:58-59).

THE BASILICA OF ST. JOHN LATERAN

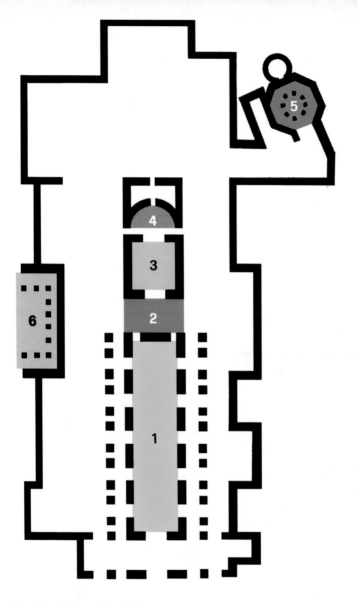

Plan of the Basilica of St. John Lateran

- 1. The Central Nave, p. 94
- 2. The Papal Altar, p. 99
- 3. The Presbytery, p. 99
- 4. The Apse, p. 99
- 5. The Baptistry, p. 103
- 6. The Cloister, p. 98

The Foundation

The Basilica of St. John Lateran, which is the Cathedral of Rome, owes its foundation to Pope Melchiades (311–314). It was built on the ruins of the huge army barracks of the *Equites Singulares,* part of the property of the family of the Plauzi Laterani. The grounds were donated to the Pope by Emperor Constantine for the purpose of building a church.

Statue of Emperor Constantine. Basilica of St. John Lateran.

Sometime during 1209 or 1210, St. Francis of Assisi came to Rome accompanied by eleven of his first brothers. They presented themselves to Pope Innocent III, who treated them harshly and sent them away, despite the recommendations of Cardinal Giovanni Colonna. Saddened by the turn of events, the friars spent the night in a nearby hospital. A short while later, Francis was summoned to the Lateran for a second time. Innocent had had a dream: before his very eyes, and without anyone putting as much as a finger on it, he witnessed the collapse of the old Lateran, the symbol of Catholicism.

In this dream, the Pope was so wrought with fear by the imagined catastrophe that he was even unable to shout. There quickly followed the appearance of a frail-looking man, who nonetheless seemed to possess gigantic strength, for he was holding up the collapsing edifice on his shoulders. At first, Innocent could see the man only from the back, but then suddenly the man turned around and looked him in the eye. Innocent saw then that he was one of the friars who had requested an apparently impossible approval that was sustained by Cardinal Colonna. During the second audience, the Pope relented and conceded "verbally" to "God's little poor one" the authorization to preach and to receive obedience from his friars.

In a dream, Innocent III sees St. Francis holding up the Basilica of St. John Lateran. From a fresco by Giotto in the upper church of the Basilica of Assisi.

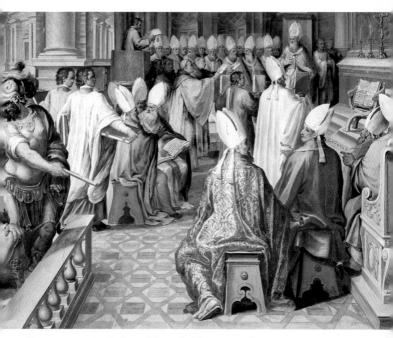

Fresco representing the Second Council of Constantinople.

During the Roman period—in fact, on the spot where this basilica can be viewed today—were the palaces of the Laterani, a powerful family which, Tacitus informs us (*Annals*, XV, 48, 56, 60), took part in the conspiracy organized by the Pisani against Emperor Nero, about A.D. 66. Unfortunately, the plot failed and the conspirators were condemned to death and their properties confiscated by the authorities. The Plauzi Laterani were able to regain possession of their properties 150 years later, only to have them expropriated again for unknown reasons. Finally, their properties came under the dominion of Emperor Constantine.

The first basilica was initially dedicated to the Savior and came to be known from these early beginnings as *Lateranense* or *Lateran* or *Aurea* (Golden). Only much later, during the pontificate of Gregory the Great (590–604), was it dedicated to St. John the Baptist and St. John the Evangelist, to both of whom was also dedicated the oratory adjacent to the baptistry.

In March and April of 1123, the first Lateran Ecumenical Council took place in this basilica. The pope at the time was Callistus II, and the decision was a result of the belief that it was no longer necessary, nor convenient, to summon ecumenical councils in the East. Subsequently, five other ecumenical councils were held in the Basilica of St. John Lateran, specifically the Councils of 1138, 1159, 1179, 1215, and the one held between 1512 and 1517.

The interior of the medieval Basilica of St. John Lateran before the Borromini renovation. Fresco by unknown artist, Church of San Martino ai Monti.

The Ancient Basilica

The Lateran Basilica was composed of five naves, but today it appears completely changed. After the Vandals of King Genseric sacked it in 455, it was restored by order of Pope Leo the Great (440–461) and later by Pope Adrian I (772–795). The sack was not the only cause of the damages inflicted upon the basilica. The effects of the earthquake of 896 induced Pope Sergius III to order its complete rebuilding in 905. Subsequently, Pope Nicholas IV (1288–1292) had it magnificently decorated. But the tormented basilica was again disfigured by a fire in 1308, which damaged irreparably some of the beautiful works of art that had adorned it through the centuries.

Clement V generously undertook its reconstruction even from the Apostolic Seat of Avignon. The work continued under Urban V (1362–1370) and then under Gregory XI (1370–1378). The Sienese artist Giovanni di Stefano was charged with the reconstruction plan.

The Present Basilica

An additional radical transformation was ordered by Innocent X (1644–1655) for the Jubilee of 1650. The Pope appointed the famous artist and architect Borromini as director. Clement XII charged the Florentine Alessandro Galilei with the complete transformation in 1735. In 1885, during the pontificate of Leo XIII, the ambulatory around the apse, a stupendous example of paleochristian art, was completely demolished in order to enlarge and renovate the apse.

Alessandro Galilei's façade appears at once as a work of art in the single order of semi-columns and Corinthian pilasters and the prominent central part. Furthermore, he intensified the beauty of the panoptical vision by placing 15 statues 7 meters high on the balustrade of the façade.

The central statue represents Christ flanked by St. John the Evangelist on one side and St. John the Baptist on the other. The remaining statues represent the Doctors of the Latin and Greek Churches. Finally, the façade was provided with an arcaded open gallery and a portico with a lintel that runs all along the façade.

The Holy Father formerly would bless the people from its central balcony, usually on Ascension Day. On the façade, there is a proud inscription, perhaps a bit excessive, which reads: "Sacrosancta Lateranensis ecclesia, omnium urbis et orbis ecclesiarum mater et caput" ("The sacrosanct Lateran Church, mother and head of all the churches of the city and of the world").

Façade of the Basilica of St. John Lateran by Alessandro Galilei.

Christ blessing the people.
Detail of the façade, Basilica of St. John Lateran.

Among the valuable works achieved by Alessandro Galilei is the barrel vault of the portico adorned with openings. From the portico, one can enter the basilica through any of five doors. The last one on the right is the Holy Door. On the left, there is a large statue of Emperor Constantine, which was found in one of his thermal baths on the Quirinale. At the center is a precious bronze door donated by the Roman Curia and modified about 1600 with the addition of contour strips that allow it to fit into the present, larger opening. Above the doors and the emperor's statue, the precious marble high reliefs reproduce some episodes from the life of St. John the Baptist.

During the excavations carried out from 1934 to 1938, important archeological artifacts, both Christian and pagan, were brought to light. Some were frescoes and others were pavement mosaics. Whole sections of paved roads were found, and of special importance, the foundations of the primitive basilica. The Lateran Palace, built by the architect Domenico Fontana in 1586,

became the Vicariate of the Diocese of Rome through the disposition of Popes John XXIII and Paul VI. The Scala Santa, the only remaining structure of the ancient papal palace, and the Triclinium constitute the last evidence of twenty centuries of history. The archeological artifacts found in the excavations are further evidence that tie this history to Nero, Constantine, and Marcus Aurelius.

An important part of this history includes the signing of the Lateran Treaty on February 11, 1929, in the palace adjacent to the basilica. The agreements between the newly formed Italian fascist government and the Church stressed that it was a way of giving "Italy to God and God to Italy."

John the Baptist, also called the Precursor, was the son of the priest Zechariah and Elizabeth. He was born six months before Christ. During his youth, he withdrew into the desert. The Holy Spirit descended upon him, after which John appeared as a prophet in Israel. He instituted a baptism of penance or spiritual transformation by

The chair of the Bishop of Rome and the apse, Basilica of St. John Lateran.

means of immersion in the waters of the river Jordan; hence the name, the Baptist. Jesus himself was baptized by John (Matt 3:15).

A commission composed of priests and levites from the sect of the Pharisees was sent to interrogate John, who answered according to the words of the prophet Isaiah (40:3), as noted by all the evangelists (Matt 3:3; Mark 1:3; Luke 3:4; John 1:23).

John's preaching was interrupted by his arrest, ordered by Herod Antipas, whom John had openly criticized for having married Herodias, the wife of his brother Philip (Matt 14:3-5). He was thrown into prison at Machaerus. His brutal death—his head on a platter—

was requested by Herodias and made possible by her daughter Salome (Matt 14:3-6).

"If you are angry with a brother or sister, you will be liable to judgment" (Matt 5:22).

"Whoever wishes to become great among you must be your servant, and whoever wishes to be first among you must be slave of all. For the Son of Man came not to be served but to serve, and to give his life a ransom for many" (Mark 10:43-45).

93

Central nave, Basilica of St. John Lateran.

The Central Nave

The central nave, with its Latin cross plan, measures 130 meters in length. The ceiling, the artistic achievement of Pirro Ligorio, was begun in 1562 by order of Pope Pius IV (1559–1565), and was completed during the pontificate of Pius V (1566–1572), who ordered its gilded finish. The imposing ornamentations were executed by Daniele da Volterra. The ceiling was later restored following the orders of Pius VI (1775–1799), who placed his coat of arms on it. Also worth noting in the central nave is the long column-shaped cosmatesque pavement completed under Martin V, the 12 niches which project from the pilasters and the columns of ancient green marble, as well as the tympanum containing the Pamphili dove.

The niches were designed by the masterful hand of Borromini, and before 1718, they contained the statues of the apostles. Above them, in stuccoed high reliefs, are scenes from the New and Old Testaments, completed by artists such as Alessandro Algardi, Antonio Raggi and Gian Francesco Rossi. Above the reliefs and between the oval frames are images of Old Testament prophets, dating from about 1718.

On the right side are statues and paintings that represent, respectively, St. Thaddeus, by Lorenzo Ottoni, and, higher up, the prophet Nahum, by Domenico M. Muratori. Following these, there is also St. Matthew, by Camillo Rusconi, and, above, the prophet Jonah, as the artist Marco Benefial imagined him. Further on, there is St. Philip, by the artist Giuseppe Nasini, and St. Thomas, by Pierre Le Gros. Above it, Hosea, attributed to Giovanni Odazzi, and following this image, that of St. James the Greater, another splendid achievement of Camillo Rusconi. Above it, there is also the prophet Ezekiel, by Gian Paolo Melchiorri. Finally, there is St. Paul, one of the many achievements of Pierre Monnot, and above it, the prophet Jeremiah, by Sebastiano Conca.

On the left side, of special importance are St. Peter, by Pierre Monnot and, above it, the prophet Isaiah, a work completed by Benedetto Luti.

Then follows St. Andrew, another work of Camillo Rusconi, and above it, the prophet Baruch by Francesco Trevisani; St. John the Evangelist, an admirable work of Camillo Rusconi, and, above, the prophet Daniel, attributed to Andrea Procaccini. Further on, there is St. James the Less, as done by Angelo de Rossi, and above it, the prophet Joel by Luigi Garzi. We can also admire St. Bartholomew, another valuable work of Pierre Le Gros, and above, the prophet Obadiah, by Giuseppe Chiari. Finally, St. Simon, by Francesco Moratti, and the prophet Micah, by Pier Leone Ghezzi, complete this cycle of images.

Baldachin, Basilica of St. John Lateran.

The Cathedral of Rome

Statue of St. John,
Basilica of St. John Lateran
(at the end of the left nave).

This cathedral possesses a strange destiny. Many Christians are unaware that it is the cathedral of Rome, as it is situated not in the center of the city but on its borders, near the Aurelian Wall. Even the Bishop of Rome, who resides in the Vatican and celebrates Mass regularly in St. Peter's, goes to St. John Lateran only two or three times a year, otherwise leaving it in the custody of his Cardinal Vicar.

Originally, the basilica was dedicated to the Savior, Christ himself, from whom, undoubtedly, was expected the salvation of the city of Rome from the barbarian invasions. Later, it was dedicated to St. John the Baptist because of the presence of the baptistry, and after that to St. John the Evangelist, for reasons which remain unclear. In any case, it is to be supposed that the dedication to St. John the Evangelist as on a par with the hierarchical power of St. Peter and St. Paul represents the spiritual intimacy without which Christian life would not exist. The "disciple that Jesus loved" is compared by Gilbert Cesbron to a poplar tree which stands erect and tall, Peter is likened to a chain, strong and solidly fixed, and Paul is similar to a walnut tree whose branches spread over a wide space.

John the Evangelist, whose heart was so close to Christ, is also the one to whom we owe the expression "God is love."

"By this everyone will know that you are my disciples, if you have love for one another" (John 13:35).

He also said, "The kingdom of God is as if someone would scatter seed on the ground, and would sleep and rise night and day, and the seed would sprout and grow, he does not know how" (Mark 4:26-27).

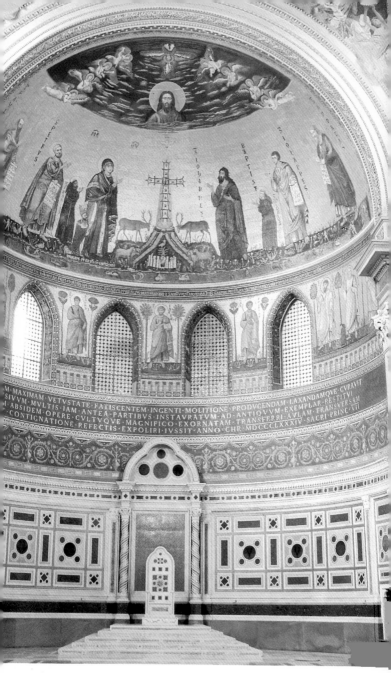

Ancient chair of the popes, preserved in the cloister of the Basilica of St. John Lateran (fourth century).

The chair of the Bishop of Rome, Basilica of St. John Lateran.

Cloister, Basilica of St. John Lateran.

The Cloister

It took seventeen years to build the cloister. It was built by the Vassallettos, as the inscription on the frieze of the front portico reveals. The dates are between 1215 and 1232, during the pontificates of Honorius III (1216–1227) and partly during that of Innocent IV (1243–1254). Small arcades on the sides rest on double columns, some of which are decorated with mosaics.

The architecture of the cloister is rich, especially the mosaic frieze and its frame, which are decorated with animal heads. The ambulatories are covered by vaults which rest on ancient columns with Ionic capitals and backed by the pilasters of the interior. They were built later, together with the arcades of the gallery above. Furthermore, the entrances' sides, which constitute the access to the passages to the courtyard, have been decorated with lions.

Along the walls of the ambulatory, one can observe the many sculptures, ornamentations, ancient inscriptions, as well as tomb slabs and varied architectural elements belonging both to the Roman and paleochristian eras

and brought to light during the excavations of the primitive basilica. To the right of the entrance, and at the beginning of the first ambulatory, are remains of the ancient baldachin. The nearby tympanums, from about 1297, are rose-shaped and contain the coat of arms of Cardinal Colonna. They are the work of Deodato. In the niches are statues of John the Evangelist and John the Baptist, the work of Capponi. They were originally on the De Pereriis altar, which was dismantled in 1492.

At the beginning of the second ambulatory are bronze door panels completed in 1196 by the artists Pietro and Umberto da Piacenza. The door panels were ordered by Celestine III (1191–1198), and later by Honorius III (1216–1227). At the middle of the fourth ambulatory is the cosmatesque seat, a work of art, composed of spiral columns and a seat belonging to the classical period.

Finally, on the corner between the first and last ambulatories, the fragments of the thirteenth-century tomb of Cardinal Annibali contain sculptural reliefs by the celebrated artist Arnolfo di Cambio.

"Turn back to the Lord and forsake your sins" (Sir 17:25).

"Those who are well have no need of a physician, but those who are sick; I have come to call not the righteous but sinners" (Mark 2:17).

Apse of the Basilica
of St. John Lateran.

The Papal Altar, Presbytery, and Apse

Restored in 1851, the papal altar is so called because only the Holy Father celebrates Mass on it. In the upper part, behind the gilded fan-windows, is preserved the precious wooden altar where the first popes—from St. Peter (64 or 67), to St. Sylvester (314–335)—celebrated their divine offices. In front, within the confessional enclosure, is the tomb of Martin V, with a bronze slab dating from about 1443 by the artist Simone Ghini. As previously noted, in 1885, Leo XIII ordered the dismantling of the ambulatory around the apse in order to enlarge and renovate the apse as well as the presbytery. The excellent work was executed by the architect Francesco Vespignani, who respected the ancient forms and, in addition, adhered to the project designed by his father Virginio. These events and people are represented on the left wall of the presbytery, where Vespignani is reproduced in the act of presenting the plan of the presbytery and apse to Pope Leo XIII.

Detail of apse, Basilica of St. John Lateran.

The Ancient Mass

"On the day that is called the day of the sun, all the inhabitants of the city and the countryside get together in the same place. A reading takes place from the Acts of the Apostles and from the books of the prophets, as long as time allows. At the end of the readings, the presider admonishes and exhorts the assembly to put into practice these teachings. Subsequently, all stand and pray out loud. Then, after the prayers are finished, they bring some bread, wine, and water. The celebrant addresses to heaven the prayers and thankful actions so that he may receive strength, and the people answer with the acclamation: Amen. Then the offering and distribution of the consecrated foods take place. All those who possess abundantly and who wish to donate may do so freely, each as he pleases. Everything which is offered is placed in the hands of the celebrant so that he may assist orphans, the aged, the sick, the poor, prisoners, foreigners and, in a word, all those who are in need."

St. Justin, *First Apology*

The first posture of Christian prayer. Cloister, Basilica of St. John Lateran.

The Unity of the Church, represented by the Christians of the first century. Cloister of the Basilica of St. John Lateran.

"During the Eucharistic mystery, give thanks.
First through the chalice:
We give thanks to thee, our Father, for
the holy vine of David, thy
servant.
Which thou revealed to us
through Jesus;
thy servant, Glory be to thee
for ever and ever!
Then, through the broken
bread:
We give thee thanks, our
Father,
for life and knowledge.
That thou revealed to us
through Jesus,
thy servant,
Glory be to thee for ever
and ever!
This broken bread
has been gathered
so that it might become one.
In the same manner,
may thy Church be united
from the ends of the earth
in thy Kingdom.
For thine is the power and
the glory.
Through Jesus Christ
for ever and ever"
(*Didache* 9).

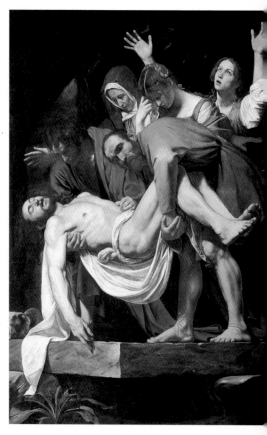

The Deposition from the Cross.
Caravaggio, Vatican Gallery.

The prized mosaic in the apse, in which the figure of the Savior stands out among the clouds and surrounded by angels, was transported from the ancient apse, restored, and placed in the cap of the apse. It is the work of the celebrated artists Iacopo Torriti and Iacopo da Camerino. In the center of the mosaic is the jeweled cross and the dove sitting on the hill that encloses the celestial Jerusalem. The four rivers which gush forth from the celestial Jerusalem are the allegorical form of the four evangelists, who will quench the thirst of God's people, represented by the sheep and the deer. On the left is the figure of Mary together with a kneeling Nicholas IV, and Sts. Peter and Paul. On the right, there are the admirable images of St. John and St. Andrew. The two smaller figures, easily traceable, are those of St. Francis, on the left, and St. Anthony of Padua, on the right. The latter were included in the clearly traditional iconographic space because Nicholas IV was so disposed, since he belonged to the Order of Friars Minor. Below, we can note the river Jordan with some figures of swan, fish and boats, while further down, there are 9 of the 12 apostles in the spaces between the windows. The two figures in the smaller spaces are the artists of the mosaic, Iacopo Torriti, on the left, and Iacopo da Camerino, on the right. Finally, on the right wall of the presbytery, are two large and splendid nineteenth-century frescoes by Francesco Grandi, representing episodes from the pontificate of Innocent III, specifically, his approval of the Dominican and Franciscan Orders.

The Place of the Celebration

The apse, also known as a "tribune," constitutes the most preeminent part of a Christian church. It is situated at the end of the central nave and contains the altar, the choir and, in a cathedral, the bishop's chair.

In referring to a church, the choir indicates a space behind the major altar to be used for music and the recitation of the sacred offices. Today, the choir may be found in the apse of the church or by the side of the presbytery.

The presbytery is the space designated for the bishop and the priests during the sacred celebrations. It is almost always present in the paleochristian basilicas, and it is situated at the end of the central nave, slightly elevated and closed by a chancel screen. It is terminated by the apse, the point at which both the bishop's chair and the priests' stone benches were placed. During the Middle Ages, the altar was placed near the wall, and the presbytery was the name given to the space before the altar where the celebrations took place.

"Do not be called double-tongued and do not lay traps with your tongue" (Sir 5:14).

"The time is fulfilled, and the kingdom of God has come near; repent, and believe in the good news" (Mark 1:15).

Baptismal font,
Basilica of St. John Lateran.

The Baptistry

The baptistry was built at the same time as the basilica to which it is adjacent. The *Liber Pontificalis* informs us that Emperor Constantine offered magnificent gifts to the basilica and the baptistry, even though he never saw it completed. Legend holds that Pope Sylvester I baptized the emperor in the Lateran baptistry. This baptistry, which is also called *San Giovanni in Fonte,* has a basin for the immersion rite situated at a level slightly lower than the pavement. At the center of the basin is an urn made of green Egyptian basalt from the end of the fourteenth century. The baptistry was probably erected by Constantine in the palace of the Laterani family. But its architecture was modified in two instances: in the fifth century, when it was redone by Sixtus III (432–440), and in 1637, when it was restored under Urban VIII and took on the form that we know today.

Due to the sanctity attached to the place, several oratories and chapels grew around it in the subsequent centuries, including: the Chapel of St. Venantius, which contains mosaics from the time of Pope John IV (640–642) and an elegant sixteenth-century wooden ceiling; the Chapel of

St. John the Evangelist, in the shape of a cross, containing mosaics from the time of Pope Hilary, the Romanesque bronze door of 1195, and a bronze statue of the saint belonging to the sixteenth century, the work of the Florentine artist Taddeo Landini; and the Chapel of the Baptist, containing a bronze door with silver crosses and epigraphs and the name of Pope Hilary inscribed on it. Finally, under the baptistry, there are traces of a Roman building thought to be the palace of the Laterani family.

Above the walls of the baptistry are paintings by Andrea Sacchi depicting episodes from the life of St. John the Baptist. Farther down on the same walls are frescoes by Andrea Camassei and Giacinto Gimignani

Baptistry, Basilica of
St. John Lateran.

representing some stories from the life of Emperor Constantine. Finally, it is important to point out *The Destruction of the Idols,* by the artist Carlo Maratta.

One of the more impressive monuments that can be viewed outside is the red granite Egyptian obelisk in the center of the square in front of the basilica. It is the tallest and most ancient of all the obelisks in the Eternal City. At its base, we can admire the splendid fountain completed in 1607.

About 435, Sixtus III had an inscription carved on the cornice of the columns, an object of meditation for all pilgrims. The inscription reads: "Generated by the Spirit who rendered these waters fecund. Here is that source of life, which cleanses the whole universe, gushing from Christ's wound. This water which receives the old man has a new man arise. There is no difference among those who are reborn. A one and only baptism, a one and only Spirit, a one and only faith: they are one."

Vault of the baptistry, Basilica of St. John Lateran.

The word "baptistry" indicates a chapel containing a baptismal font. It is usually adjacent to a cathedral. The first Christians were baptized in springs, in rivers, in lakes, and even in the sea. When the Christian Church began to consolidate and extend itself, large baptismal baths were built in porticos or in other suitable parts of the church. Hence, the origin of baptistries in the proximity of the churches, where the catechumens could be instructed and baptized by means of immersion. Later, niches and tabernacles containing baptismal fonts were built in more isolated areas within the churches. The oldest baptistry in Italy is that of St. John Lateran.

Detail of the mosaic in the chapel of the baptistry, Basilica of St. John Lateran.

The LORD is my shepherd, I shall
    not want.
  He makes me lie down in
    green pastures;
he leads me beside still waters;
  he restores my soul.
He leads me in right paths
  for his name's sake.

Even though I walk through the
    darkest valley,
  I fear no evil;
for you are with me;
  your rod and your staff—
    they comfort me.

You prepare a table before me
  in the presence of my enemies;
you anoint my head with oil;
  my cup overflows.

Surely goodness and mercy
    shall follow me
  all the days of my life,
and I shall dwell in the house of
    the LORD
  my whole life long.
                              (Psalm 23)

Detail of the mosaic in the chapel of the
baptistry, Basilica of St. John Lateran.

THE BASILICA OF ST. MARY MAJOR (SANTA MARIA MAGGIORE)

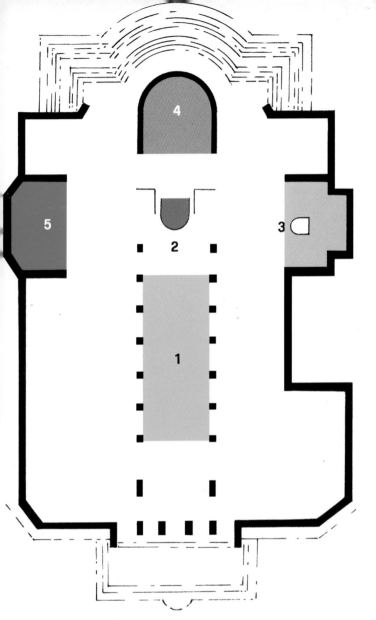

Plan of the Basilica of St. Mary Major

1. The Central Nave, p. 113
2. The Confession, p. 116
3. The Chapel of the Blessed Sacrament, p. 114
4. The Apse, p. 116
5. The Pauline Chapel, p. 118

The Miracle

This basilica owes its beginnings to a miracle. During the night of August 4, 352, Pope St. Liberius and Giovanni, a rich citizen, saw an immense cross in the sky. The following morning (August 5), a miraculous snowfall covered the precise spot on which the basilica would be situated. For this reason, it was first called *Santa Maria ad Nives* (St. Mary of the Snows), then Santa Maria Liberiana. Before the sixth century, it was also known as *Santa Maria ad Praesepe*, since the remains of the manger where the baby Jesus had been laid had been previously brought to this basilica. Finally, it was called Santa Maria Maggiore because it is the largest of the 26 churches consecrated to the Mother of God in Rome. Nonetheless, according to the *Liber Pontificalis*, the construction of the basilica is attributed to Sixtus III (432–440), who wished to consecrate it to the Madonna after the Council of Ephesus (June 7, 431) established that Mary could be called Mother of God, *Theotokos*.

Nicholas IV (1288–1292) ordered the renovation of the apse, and Clement X (1670–1676), the principal façade. Between the fifth and eighteenth centuries, the original plan underwent various modifications and additions: the transept and new apse (1200); the *Oratorium ad Praesepe* (1290); the portico's mosaics (1300); the bell tower, the highest in Rome (75 meters), in 1377; the lacunar ceiling by Giuliano da Sangallo (end of 1400); drawings of the Sforza Chapel by Michelangelo, subsequently reelaborated by Giacomo della Porta (1564–1573); the Chapel of the Blessed Sacrament (1605–1611); and, finally, the canopy of the main altar, and the monumental façade, belonging to the middle of 1700.

The bell tower of the Basilica of St. Mary Major, the highest bell tower in Rome. Anonymous artist of the eighteenth century. Museo di Roma, Palazzo Braschi.

The name "Mary" probably has its origins in Egyptian. In the language of the pharaohs, the word *myr* means "the loved one." The Israelites added the Hebrew suffix *jam*, which means "God." The result was *Myriam*, that is, "the one loved by God."

Mosaic of the Virgin Mary and Child. Basilica of St. Mary Major.

The Annunciation: Roger van der Weyden. Louvre, Paris.

Mary is the Virgin Mother of Jesus Christ. With the free consent of her faith, and under the influence of grace, Mary conceived the Son of God, and gave him that existence from her very womb which made it possible for Christ to become a member of the human race as well as its Redeemer (Matt 1:18-23; Luke 1:26-38). As a result of the hypostatic union of the Son of God with the human nature conceived by her—that is, permanent union and unity in one person—Mary is "the Mother of the Lord" (Luke 1:43), that is to say, *Theotokos*.

The dome of the Basilica of St. Mary Major.

The triumphal arch, Basilica of St. Mary Major.

Virgin Mother, daughter of thy son; humble beyond all creatures and more exalted; predestined turning point of God's intention; Thy merit so ennobled human nature that its divine Creator did not scorn to make Himself the creature of his creature. The Love that was kindled in thy womb sends forth the warmth of the eternal peace within whose ray this flower has come to bloom. Here, to us, thou art the noon and scope of Love revealed; and among mortal men, the living fountain of eternal hope. Lady, thou art so near God's reckonings that who seeks grace and does not first seek thee would have his wish fly upward without wings. Not only does thy sweet beneficence flow out to all who beg, but oftentimes thy charity arrives before the plea. In thee is pity, in thee munificence, in thee the tenderest heart, in thee unites all that creation knows of excellence!

(Dante Alighieri, *Paradiso;* Canto XXXIII, vv. 1-21)

The Central Nave

The pavement is decorated with disks of serpentine and porphyry, the work of the Cosmati masters. The columns which divide the spaces are connected by a lintel made of brick and covered with stucco. The first load of gold arriving in Spain from the New World was fused to make the gold leaves used in decorating the ceiling. Giuliano da Sangallo made the pontifical coat of arms of Alexander VI Borgia (1492–1503).

The mosaics in the central nave represent, on the left wall, scenes from the life of Moses and Joshua. Of the 42 mosaic panels that were here originally, only 27 remain, and they are not all by the same hand. The 12 panels on the left wall, and those on the right wall, do not possess a unifying theme or subject, but are independent of each other. Of the 12 panels which today are on the left wall, 3 refer to the story of Abraham and 9 to Jacob.

"O glorious Lady, high above the stars, you nourish on your bosom the God who created you. Through your Son you give us back the joy which Eve took away from us, and disclose the journey toward the heavens. You are the path to peace and the celestial gate. May the world redeemed by your Son acclaim you. Glory and praise to God the Father, to the Son and to the Holy Spirit that have adorned you with the mantle of grace. Amen."

The Nicaean Council, Vatican Museums (Vatican Library, Greco 1613 f. 108).

113

Chapel of the Blessed Sacrament, Basilica of St. Mary Major.

The Chapel of the Blessed Sacrament or Chapel of Sixtus V

This chapel is named after Pope Sixtus V (1520–1590), who commissioned its construction. It was begun in 1585 by Domenico Fontana. The plan is that of a Greek cross topped with an ample cupola that sits on a high drum and is decorated with frescoes made by various mannerist artists at the end of the sixteenth century and restored in 1870. At the center of the altar is the gilded ciborium in the shape of a small temple made by Ludovico Scalzo. It is sustained by four bronze angels by Barolomeo Torrigiani on the basis of a drawing by G.B. Ricci (1590).

On the level below is the *Oratorium ad Praesepe*, the chapel belonging to the high Middle Ages, renovated by

Arnolfo di Cambio (c. 1289) and placed in this spot by Domenico Fontana. The parts of Arnolfo's work which remain include the David and Isaiah in the pendentives of the entrance arch, inside, the Magi, St. Joseph, the ox and donkey in the frontal of the altar. The Madonna is from the sixteenth century, and the pavement is made of mosaic. The tomb of St. Pius V, by Domenico Fontana, is in the left wing of the chapel. The statue of the Pope is the work of Leonardo Sormani (1587), and the five bas-reliefs with scenes of his pontificate are by N. Pippi and Egidio della Riviera. On the sides are St. Peter Martyr, by Leonardo Sormani, and St. Dominic, by G.B. della

Porta. The tomb of Sixtus V, by Domenico Fontana, is situated in the right arm. The Pope's statue is by Valsoldo, and the five bas-reliefs with scenes of his pontificate are by the same Valsoldo, N. Pippi and E. della Riviera. In the side niches we see St. Francis, by Flaminio Vacca, and St. Anthony, by P.P. Olivieri. In the niches of the far wing are statues of St. Peter and St. Paul by Prospero Bresciano and Valsoldo.

"The shepherds heard hymns in praise of the coming of the incarnated Christ, and ran to see the shepherd. They saw the immaculate Lamb nourish himself from Mary's bosom, and they celebrated her in these words:

Hail, O Mother of the Lamb and of the shepherd; hail sheepfold of the mystical flock.

Hail, protection from invisible enemies; hail, passage to the doors of heaven.

Hail, because the celestial spheres are rejoicing with the earth; hail, because the earth rejoices with the heavens.

Hail, perennial voice of the apostles; hail, unconquerable courage of athletes.

Hail, unshaken foundation of faith; hail, splendid sign of grace.

Hail, You through whom hell was stripped; hail, You through whom we were covered with glory.

Hail, O unblemished Bride."

(Hymn Akathistos, of the Byzantine liturgy, Second Station).

The Nativity, Chapel of the Blessed Sacrament, Basilica of St. Mary Major.

The cap of the apse, Basilica of St. Mary Major.

The Confession and the Apse

The confession (a shrine with relics below an altar) was built according to a drawing of Virginio Vespignano (1864). The statue of Pius IX kneeling is by Ignazio Iacometti (about 1880). Ferdinando Fuga is the artist who completed the canopy over the principal altar, which is sustained by four porphyry columns enveloped in bronze leaves. The urn, also made of porphyry, contains the relics of the apostle Matthew as well as those of other martyrs. Light enters the apse through four windows in the form of pointed arches. For this reason, this is one of the first examples of Gothic architecture in Rome. Nicholas IV (1288–1292) chose the Franciscan Iacopo Torriti to carry out the decoration, and he completed the work in 1295. In the center of the large circle, the two large figures represent

"Eternal Word, who has elected Mary as the incorruptible ark of thy abode, blessed be Thou!

Our Redeemer, who has rendered Mary the most holy sanctuary of the Holy Spirit, blessed be Thou!

King of kings, who has exalted Mary through the Assumption into heaven of her body and soul, blessed be Thou!

Lord of heaven and earth, who has crowned Mary Queen of the universe, and has placed her at thy right hand, blessed be Thou!" (Invocation for the feast of the Assumption of the Blessed Virgin Mary).

Marble tomb of Cardinal Consalvo Rodriguez, Archbishop of Toledo, Basilica of St. Mary Major. ➡

the Redeemer enthroned in the act of crowning his Mother and, on each side of the throne, nine angels. On the left, are St. Peter, St. Paul, St. Francis, and Pope Nicholas IV, kneeling. On the right, the saints depicted are St. John the Baptist, St. John the Evangelist, and St. Anthony. The kneeling figure is Cardinal Giacomo Colonna. At the end of the right arm of the transept is the marble tomb of Cardinal Consalvo Rodriguez, Archbishop of Toledo and Bishop of Albano, who died in 1299. In 1705, Cardinal Albani had the tomb transferred to the end of the right nave of the church, near the door that opens onto the Piazza Esquilino. The work is by Giovanni Cosma. At the top of the Gothic arch, the Virgin enthroned is represented in a mosaic. She is surrounded by St. Matthew and St. Jerome while the cardinal is kneeling in prayer. Encased in the wall in the lower part of the apse's circle, there are four bas-reliefs, which were originally in the ancient balduchin of the papal altar. They are the work of Mino del Reame (1474?), and include *The Nativity* and *Miracle of the Snow* on the left, and *The Assumption* and *The Epiphany* on the right. The canvas with the *Nativity* is the work of Francesco Mancini.

The Pauline or Borghese Chapel

The name of this chapel derives from the Pope who commissioned it, Paul V Borghese. In 1605, the project was assigned to Flaminio Ponzio, who adopted the architectural plan of Fontana and completed it in 1611. Nonetheless, the Pauline Chapel, contrary to the Chapel of Sixtus V, conceived in the style of the sixteenth century or the Renaissance, reveals a clear tendency toward baroque architecture. Prophets and sibyls are represented in the pendentives of the cupola, while in the large lunette above the altar is the Apparition of the Madonna and of St. John the Evangelist to St. Gregory Thaumaturgus. The frescoes are the work of Cavalier d'Arpino. In the cupola, are the "Madonna and the Apostles" by Cigoli (1612).

Basing himself on the drawings of Girolamo Rainaldi and Tempesti (1611), Pompeo Targoni completed the altar ornated with jasper, agate, amethyst and lapis lazuli. On the frontispiece are bronze angels, by Camillo Mariani, and Pope Liberius, who signs the plan of the basilica, a marble relief by Stefano Maderno. In the center is a sumptuous frame made of angels unfolding the image of the *Madonna Sancta Maria ad Nives*. The frame is the work of Camillo Mariani, while the image is of Byzantine origin, attributed to St. Luke by tradition. The image is also known as the *Salus Populi Romani* for the exceptional devotion which the people of Rome have for this image of the Virgin. On the sides of the altar, there are statues of St. John the Evangelist and St. Joseph, by Camillo Mariani and Ambrogio Buonvicino.

At the end of the left arm of the chapel is the tomb of Paul V by Flaminio Ponzio. The statue of the Pope is by Silla da Viggiù. The bas-reliefs in the lower part, with scenes from the pontificate, are by Camillo Mariani and Buonvicino. The bas-reliefs above are by Antonio Valsoldo, Buzio, and Cristoforo Stati. On the sides are statues of David and St. Athanasius by Cordier. Around the top are other frescoes that represent stories of St. Francis, St. Dominic, and others by Guido Reni (1613). In the right wing, there is the tomb of Clement VIII by Ponzio. The statue of the Pope in the act of blessing is by Silla da Viggiù. The bas-reliefs with scenes of the pontificate are by Mariani, Buzio, Pietro Bernini (the father of Giovanni Lorenzo), and Antonio Valsoldo. On the sides, we see Aaron and St. Bernard, by Nicolas Cordier.

The Pauline or Borghese Chapel.
Madonna Sancta Maria ad Nives,
Basilica of St. Mary Major.

The Pauline or Borghese Chapel. *Madonna Sancta Maria ad Nives,*
Basilica of St. Mary Major. Detail.

"Salve, Regina, mater misericordiae; vita, dulcedo et spes nostra, salve. Ad te clamamus, éxsules filii Evae. Ad te suspiramus, geméntes et flentes in hac lacrimarum valle. Eia ergo, advocata nostra, illos tuos misericordes oculos ad nos convérte. Et Iesum, benedictum fructum ventris tui, nobis post hoc exsilium osténde."

"Hail, Holy Queen, Mother of Mercy. Our life, our sweetness and our hope! To you do we cry, poor ban-ished children of Eve. To you do we send up our sighs; mourning and weeping in this vale of tears. Turn then, most gracious Advocate, your eyes of mercy toward us; and after this, our exile, show unto us the blessed fruit of your womb, Jesus. O clement, O loving, O sweet Virgin Mary. Pray for us, O holy Mother of God. That we may be made worthy of the promises of Christ.")

The Popes

St. Peter (64–67)
St. Linus, M. (67–76)
St. Anacletus or
    Cletus, M. (76–88)
St. Clement, I, M. (88–97)
St. Evaristus, M. (97–105)
St. Alexander I, M. (105–115)
St. Sixtus I, M. (115–125)
St. Telesphorus, M. (125–136)
St. Hyginus, M. (136–140)
St. Pius I, M. (140–155)
St. Anicetus, M. (155–166)
St. Soterus, M. (166–175)
St. Eleuterius, M. (175–189)
St. Victor I, M. (189–199)
St. Zephyrinus, M. (199–217)
St. Callistus I, M. (217–222)
St. Urban I, M. (222–230)
St. Pontian, M. (230–235)
St. Anterus, M. (235–236)
St. Fabian, M. (236–250)
St. Cornelius, M. (251–253)
St. Lucius I, M. (253–254)
St. Stephen I, M. (254–257)
St. Sixtus II, M. (257–258)
St. Dionysius (259–268)
St. Felix I, M. (269–274)
St. Eutychian, M. (275–283)
St. Caius, M. (283–296)
St. Marcellinus, M. (296–304)
St. Marcellus I, M. (308–309)
St. Eusebius, M. (309)
St. Melchiades, M. (311–314)
St. Sylvester I (314–335)
St. Mark (336)
St. Julius I (337–352)
Liberius (352–366)
St. Damasus I (366–384)
St. Siricius (384–399)
St. Anastasius I (399–401)
St. Innocent I (401–417)
St. Zozimus (417–418)
St. Boniface I (418–422)
St. Celestine I (422–432)
St. Sixtus III (432–440)
St. Leo I (the Great) (440–461)
St. Hilary (461–468)
St. Simplicius (468–483)

St. Felix III or II (483–492)
St. Gelasius I (492–496)
Anastasius II (496–498)
St. Symmachus (498–514)
St. Hormisdas (514–523)
St. John I (523–526)
St. Felix IV or III (526–530)
Boniface II (530–532)
John II (533–535)
St. Agapitus II (535–536)
St. Silverius, M. (536–537)
Vigilius (537–555)
Pelagius I (556–561)
John III (561–574)
Benedict I (575–579)
Pelagius II (579–590)
St. Gregory I (the Great)
    (590–604)
Sabinianus (604–606)
Boniface III (607)
St. Boniface IV (608–615)
St. Deusdeditus or
    Adeodatus I (615–618)
Boniface V (619–625)
Honorius I (625–638)
Severinus (640)
John IV (640–642)
Theodore I (642–649)
St. Martin I, M. (649–655)
St. Eugene I (654–657)
St. Vitalian (657–672)
Adeodatus II (672–676)
Donus (676–678)
St. Agathonus (678–681)
St. Leo II (682–683)
St. Benedict II (684–685)
John V (685–686)
Conon (686–687)
St. Sergius I (687–701)
John VI (701–705)
John VII (705–707)
Sisinnius (708)
Constantine (708–715)
St. Gregory II (715–731)
St. Gregory III (731–741)
St. Zachary (741–752)
Stephen II (752–757)
St. Paul I (757–767)

Stephen III (768–772)
Adrian I (772–795)
St. Leo III (795–816)
Stephen IV (816–817)
St. Paschal I (817–824)
Eugene II (824–827)
Valentine (827)
Gregory IV (827–844)
Sergius II (844–847)
St. Leo IV (847–855)
Benedict III (855–858)
St. Nicholas I (the Great)
    (858–867)
Adrian II (867–872)
John VIII (872–882)
Marinus I (882–884)
St. Adrian III (884–885)
Stephen V (885–891)
Formosus (891–896)
Boniface VI (896)
Stephen VI (896–897)
Romanus (897)
Theodore II (897)
John IX (898–900)
Benedict IV (900–903)
Leo V (903)
Sergius III (904–911)
Anastasius III (911–913)
Landus (913–914)
John X (914–928)
Leo VI (928)
Stephen VII (928–931)
John XI (931–935)
Leo VII (936–939)
Stephen VIII (939–942)
Marinus II (942–946)
Agapitus II (946–955)
John XII (955–964)
Leo VIII (963–965)
Benedict V (964–966)
John XIII (965–972)
Benedict VI (973–974)
Benedict VII (974–983)
John XIV (983–984)
John XV (985–996)
Gregory V (996–999)
Sylvester II (999–1003)
John XVII (1003)

John XVIII (1004–1009)
Sergius IV (1009–1012)
Benedict VIII (1012–1024)
John XIX (1024–1032)
Benedict IX (1032–1044)
Sylvester III (1045)
Benedict IX (1045)
Gregory VI (1045–1046)
Clement II (1046–1047)
Benedict IX (1047–1048)
Damasus II (1048)
St. Leo IX (1048–1054)
Victor II (1055–1057)
Stephen IX (1057–1058)
Nicholas II (1059–1061)
Alexander II (1061–1073)
St. Gregory VII (1073–1085)
B. Victor III (1086–1087)
B. Urban II (1088–1099)
Paschal II (1099–1118)
Gelasius II (1118–1119)
Callistus II (1119–1124)
Honorius II (1124–1130)
Innocent II (1130–1143)
Celestine II (1143–1144)
Lucius II (1144–1145)
B. Eugene III (1145–1153)
Anastasius IV (1153–1154)
Adrian IV (1154–1159)
Alexander III (1159–1181)
Lucius III (1181–1185)
Urban III (1185–1187)
Gregory VIII (1187)
Clement III (1187–1191)
Celestine III (1191–1198)
Innocent III (1198–1216)
Honorius III (1216–1227)
Gregory IX (1227–1241)
Celestine IV (1241)
Innocent IV (1243–1254)
Alexander IV (1254–1261)
Urban IV (1261–1264)
Clement IV (1265–1268)
B. Gregory X (1271–1276)
B. Innocent V (1276)
Adrian V (1276)
John XXI (1276–1277)
Nicholas III (1277–1280)

St. Peter and St. Paul. Fragment of a cup. Vatican Museums.

Martin IV (1281–1285)
Honorius IV (1285–1287)
Nicholas IV (1288–1292)
St. Celestine V (1294)
Boniface VIII (1294–1303)
B. Benedict XI (1303–1304)
Clement V (1305–1314)
John XXII (1316–1334)
Benedict XII (1334–1342)
Clement VI (1342–1352)
Innocent VI (1352–1362)
B. Urban V (1362–1370)
Gregory XI (1370–1378)
Urban VI (1378–1389)
Boniface IX (1389–1404)
Innocent VII (1404–1406)
Gregory XII (1406–1415)
Martin V (1417–1431)
Eugene IV (1431–1447)

Nicholas V (1447–1455)
Callistus III (1455–1458)
Pius II (1458–1464)
Paul II (1464–1471)
Sixtus IV (1471–1484)
Innocent VIII (1484–1492)
Alexander VI (1492–1503)
Pius III (1503)
Julius II (1503–1513)
Leo X (1513–1521)
Adrian VI (1522–1523)
Clement VII (1523–1534)
Paul III (1534–1549)
Julius III (1550–1555)
Marcellus II (1555)
Paul IV (1555–1559)
Pius IV (1559–1565)
St. Pius V (1566–1572)
Gregory XIII (1572–1585)

Sixtus V (1585–1590)
Urban VII (1590)
Gregory XIV (1590–1591)
Innocent IX (1591)
Clement VIII (1592–1605)
Leo XI (1605)
Paul V (1605–1621)
Gregory XV (1621–1623)
Urban VIII (1623–1644)
Innocent X (1644–1655)
Alexander VII (1655–1667)
Clement IX (1667–1669)
Clement X (1670–1676)
B. Innocent XI (1676–1689)
Alexander VIII (1689–1691)
Innocent XII (1691–1700)
Clement XI (1700–1721)
Innocent XIII (1721–1724)
Benedict XIII (1724–1730)

Clement XII (1730–1740)
Benedict XIV (1740–1758)
Clement XIII (1758–1769)
Clement XIV (1769–1774)
Pius VI (1775–1799)
Pius VII (1800–1823)
Leo XII (1823–1829)
Pius VIII (1829–1830)
Gregory XVI (1831–1846)
Pius IX (1846–1878)
Leo XIII (1878–1903)
St. Pius X (1903–1914)
Benedict XV (1914–1922)
Pius XI (1922–1939)
Pius XII (1939–1958)
John XXIII (1958–1963)
Paul VI (1963–1978)
John Paul I (1978)
John Paul II (1978–)

Useful Information

Emergency Telephone Numbers
Police **113**
Ambulance **5510 (113)**
Fire department **115**
State police **112**
Car breakdowns **116**
　　　(ACI-Automobile Club of Italy)

Reminder of Rules and Regulations

All churches are open from dawn to sunset. It is necessary to dress properly in order to be allowed in any of the basilicas. Access is forbidden if one is wearing shorts, miniskirts, or garments that leave shoulders or waistlines bare. It is forbidden to walk around the interior of churches during Mass or other ceremonies. Finally, it is necessary to observe all posted rules regarding the use of cameras.

Roman Forum.

Papal Audiences

Requests to attend the Pope's general audiences should be addressed to the *Prefettura della Casa Pontificia (00120 - Vatican City - Telephone Extension: 6988)* at least two days before but not more than a month preceding the date of the audience.

Public Transportation

The Subway System (or Metro)

The subway system comprises three lines: A, B, and C; this third line is under construction.

The A line, Anagnina-Ottaviano, has the following stops: *Cinecittà, Subaugusta, G. Agricola, L. Sestino, N. Quadrato, P. Furba, Arco di Travertino, C. Albani, F. Camillo, Pontelungo, Re di Roma, S. Giovanni (useful stop for the Basilica of St. John Lateran), Manzoni, Piazza Vittorio, Termini (railway station), Repubblica, Barberini, Piazza di Spagna, Flaminio, Lepanto, Ottaviano/S. Pietro (useful stop for St. Peter's).*

The Trevi Fountain.

The B line, Laurentina Rebibbia, has the following stops: *Laurentina, Eur Fermi, Palasport, Magliana, Marconi, Basilica of St. Paul Outside the Walls, Garbatella, Termini (railway station), C.C. Pretorio, Policlinico, Bologna, Tiburtina FS (railway station—trains for Fiumicino Airport), M. Tiburtini, Pietralata, S.M. del Soccorso, Rebibbia.*

The subways entrances and exits are indicated by a large, red M. A map of the subway network and its stops is posted in every station. The trains run from 5:30 a.m. to midnight.

The Bus System

Most artistic monuments are reachable by the bus system. A single ticket covers 75 minutes of travel on any number of buses. Tickets must be bought before boarding the buses, and they are on sale in most bars, newspaper stands, tobacco shops, or at the ATAC main office in Piazza dei Cinquecento, the large square in front of the Termini station, which also serves as the largest bus depot. Tickets must be stamped upon boarding the bus. Every bus has a stamping machine located near the entrance door at the back of the bus.

Some important bus routes include: 23 (Termini, Trastevere, Basilica of St. Paul Outside the Walls; 27 (Termini, Roman Forum, Colosseum, Piramide); 64 (Termini, Piazza Venezia, Piazza Navona, St. Peter's); 75 (Termini, Piazza Venezia, Trastevere); 81 (Colosseum, Piazza Argentina, Lungotevere, Piazza Risorgimento—Vatican Museums); 93 (Termini, Basilica of St. Mary Major, Terme di Caracalla, Eur Fermi); 95 (Piazza Venezia, Via del Tritone, Via Veneto, Piazzale Flaminio, Piazza del Popolo).

Thanks to all those who have made possible the completion of this volume: Luciano Buccino, Ariane de Saint Marq, Madeline Diener, Paolo Gianni, André Held, Mons. D. J. Lewis, Alfio Maria Pergolizzi (Director of the Photographic Archives of the Fabbrica di San Pietro), Emanuela Pompili, Mauro Pucciarelli, Cristian Riehl, Nelly Rodriguez, Marjorie Weeke (Delegate of the Audiovisual Services, Vatican City), Pontifical Administration of the Basilica of St. Paul Outside the Walls, Pontifical Administration of St. John Lateran, Pontifical Administration of the Basilica of St. Mary Major.